# THE BU$INESS UNLOCK

## THE SYSTEM FOR PREDICTABLE SCALE

### RAJ JHA

*The Business Unlock: The System for Predictable Scale*

©2024 by Raj Jha

Printed in the United States of America

Paperback: ISBN: 979-8-9916194-0-0
Ebook: ISBN: 979-8-9916194-1-7

Library of Congress Control Number: pending

To Mom, who taught me to appreciate
and learn from the past.

To Dad, who taught me to live for today
and build for tomorrow.

# CONTENTS

# PREFACE

**Most business books disrespect the reader.** We plow through 300 pages of redundant examples, stories we don't care about, and the author stroking his ego – when the book could have been a blog post.

I wrote this to give you an easy-to-digest instruction manual for your business, delivered in the most practical way possible.

Here's what you'll discover:

- You'll (finally) truly understand WHY things happen in your company,
- You'll discover a consistent way of diagnosing problems,
- You'll understand the growth levers at your disposal, and
- You'll future-proof your company.

Most business books are about solutions that worked once. This book is about solutions that *always* work – universal principles that enable companies to survive and thrive. They're like Newton's laws. It doesn't matter where you live or when you live, force is always going to equal the product of mass and acceleration.

I've used the principles in these pages to advise micro-businesses and Fortune 100 companies. I've used them to start, grow (and find solutions to painful problems in) five of my own businesses.

It's the book I wished I had 30 years ago when I started my career.

… and in just a few pages I'll give you a map to jump around to the parts of this book that will make the biggest difference for you *right now*.

# ACKNOWLEDGMENTS

This book wouldn't be without the support of some amazing people –

My wife Dawn, without whom most of the best things in my life would never have come true.

My daughters Jackie and Amelia remind me daily what is really important.

My friend and colleague Joel Widmer, my sounding board for over a decade.

My Chief of Staff Ally Rodriguez gives me more space to think and do my best work than at any point in my career.

Ellen Fishbein and Dr. William Jaworski of Altamira Studio who were instrumental in helping me shape and communicate the ideas in this book in a way I never thought possible.

# MY BUSINESS SUCKED.

"I should just shut it down and walk away," I said.

Tom listened for a moment.

"You're making money! Looks like you're doing great to me."

Tom had never run a business. Expecting a normie to understand a founder's problems was pointless.

New day, different shitshow – that was my marketing agency. Everything felt out of control. An account manager would screw something up, and I'd parachute in to fix it. A sales rep was busy *not* logging deals in the CRM so later in the month I'd have no idea what the pipeline was. Customers were churning as fast as we added them, and my inbox was an endless litany of complaints. I had trouble sleeping, and even when I could sleep, I'd wake up wondering what grenade I'd have to jump on today.

I thought I had a management problem, so I hired a full-time head of operations. She lasted three months and spent most of her time organizing a coup to take the staff and client base with her.

What the fuck was wrong?!

The truth was, I didn't have a real business: I couldn't take a break, and though I didn't have a spare minute to think about it, the business was unsellable.

I didn't think there was a way out. But there was. I just needed to remember two things I'd learned as a child.

The first was a game called Water Works – the "Leaky Pipe Card Game".

There was a deck of cards with different kinds of pipes on it. The pipes were at different angles, had different branches and connectors, were made of different materials … and some leaked. To win the game you would build a complicated network of pipes.

But there was a rule: if water couldn't flow through a pipe, the only move you were allowed to make was to fix that leak before continuing.

In our entrepreneurial life, we don't have that limitation. We can keep building a business with a ton of leaks, and deal with them later. And for startups that's a good thing, because in the early stages of a business cutting corners is often the only way to make progress.

The problem is that as the business grows we get *used to* leaky pipes. Every founder tolerates 'leaks' in the early days because he has to. I'd let sales documentation be less than perfect because when I did sales myself, the know-how was all in my head. But four full-time sales reps later, the in-the-head approach wasn't working.

Inertia keeps us accepting leaks far longer than we should if we want to grow. As you'll see in this book not only will these leaks prevent a business from growing, but they be devastating on valuation when you want to sell it.

So how do we fix the leaks?

Twelve-year-old Raj didn't know it, but he also had the model for solving a leaking business sitting across the room from his Water Works game. Because he was a geek.

My parents had gotten the most magic object I've ever owned – An Apple ][+ computer. So beautifully primitive it didn't even have lower case letters, but that didn't matter.

I spent countless hours making the machine do my bidding. In those hours I wasn't the most awkward, least-cool pre-teen in town – I was creating my own universe. Coding on a primitive computer taught me something I used through high school, college, law school, two careers, and starting five businesses – for most of that time, without articulating it:

A machine – any machine – can be described in a simple way that clarifies how it works, what's wrong with it, and how to make it better.

What I'd forgotten in my marketing agency was that every business is a machine. I should have remembered Water Works and my Apple ][+.

**I'd forgotten the business was a *system*, and systems can be modeled like any machine.**

When you start building a beginner's machine, like a go-cart, it's fine that everything is a little loose. The steering kind of sucks, the wheels aren't aligned. But fast forward a few years and you're barrelling down a highway in that same go-cart – and now it has a V-6 – but you never had time to install a suspension system, the shaking is giving you a headache, the wood screws holding together the chassis are coming loose … and your butt hurts.

Some entrepreneurs can suck it up for long periods of time. They either have no solutions and just live with the problems, or they use makeshift solutions as a band-aid. Just drill in another wood screw to hold the joint that's failing. But as soon as conditions change (e.g. customer expectations, technology), the whole thing starts failing again. Then they come up with a new tactic that hopefully, maybe, works.

What they lack is an overall strategy for diagnosing and solving problems. A way to upgrade the machine, bit by bit, in a way that makes sense.

When we don't model our business that way, it becomes witchcraft. We don't know why the machine is broken, so we hunt for One Magic Incantation that will fix it. We spend hours doomscrolling YouTube videos hoping the Business Guru De Jour will just give us that piece of information we're missing.

> If your business isn't behaving the way you expect (or want), it isn't *one* missing piece of information. It's that you're not operating the business as a *system* that can make results repeatable.

Last year my car's check engine light came on unhelpfully alerting me that "something" was wrong. Unfortunately, my excellent 78-year-old Japanese mechanic who cursed at me incessantly even though I was a great customer had just passed away.

No mechanic, so what to do? Most people, if they couldn't take their car in to check what was wrong, would drive around with the check engine light on until the motor seized. Then they'd walk away abandoning the car.

Fortunately, I have what's called an On-Board Diagnostics (OBD) scanner. It's a little device that lets me read the logs from the car's computer. I plugged it in, and it told me I had two air injection system failures.

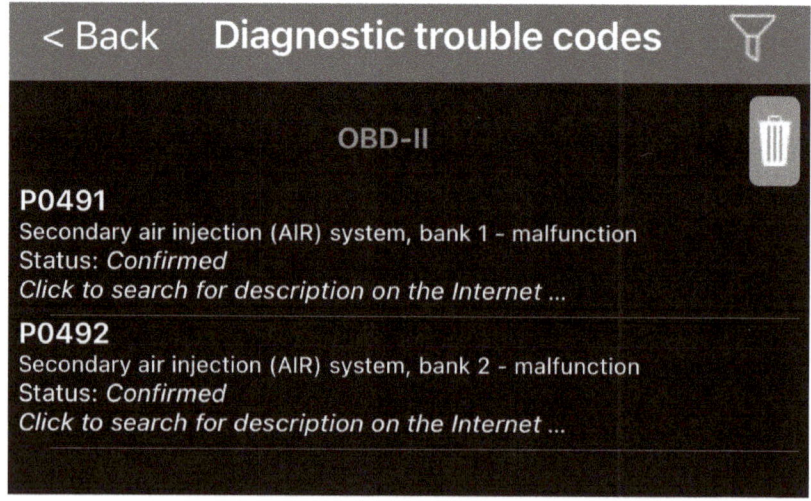

Because I knew this kind of problem wasn't one of the famous engine-destroying "factory grenades" that Porsche pre-installs as a favor to its loyal customers, I could continue driving without worrying about it. I could also discuss the problem intelligently with my new mechanic, an equally skilled Albanian who tells me he can't go back to the state of Florida again unless he wants to be arrested.

Here's the point: a car is a magic machine for most people. When it breaks down and you bring it to the mechanic, does he pull out his book of spells? Doomscroll on YouTube looking for a fix-it guru who will have the answer? Does he just hope and pray for things to get better?

No, he pulls out the service manual where someone has painstakingly diagrammed out every aspect of the vehicle. He knows what diagnostics to check, what experiments to run to isolate the problem, then what parts (or sub-parts) to repair or replace.

Because I knew there was a manual, which problems were important and which weren't, and I could check the logs to see which kinds of problems there were, handling it was easier for me.

It's the same thing for your business – but unlike a car, you built it. It's possible for you to not only have an understanding of how it works, but a service manual, and diagnostics to check.

In my agency, stressed out and wanting to shut it down and walk away, I'd forgotten that. It took a year of lifting, but on the other side we had processes documented, were tracking performance, a sellable business, and life was much, much better.

As you read this book, you'll find solving problems isn't as confusing as you feared. You'll find that upgrading the business is easier (supercharger, anyone?).

That's the Business Unlock.

# What's In This Book

This book contains a *single* methodology for understanding your business and taking control of it. It'll help you diagnose problems and formulate reliable strategies for growth.

Most business books treat different departments differently. They'll treat marketing differently from finance. On the surface level, that seems to make sense – how could these two be similar?

**The better question:** what if there's a *single architecture* at every level of a company?

Once you see that architecture, you can't unsee it. And you can solve problems and make optimizations in one department in the same way you solve problems and make optimizations in others.

Here's why this is important to you:

1. **You'll understand your business better.** That means you'll understand why your company is behaving the way it is.
2. **You'll discover a consistent way of diagnosing problems.** The issues in your business are only going to get worse. Problems are like Gremlins when they get wet – they spawn more of them.[1] You can fix problems using a single methodology.

---

1   Don't like 80's references? Sorry, find another book.

3. **You'll finally optimize your operations.** The right way to optimize isn't simply to get a new tool and give it to whoever is in charge of that department. The right way to do it is to understand how the business is constructed before choosing tools.

4. **You'll future-proof your business.** The process will put your company at the frontier of adopting technology, including AI, to supercharge it. You'll not only solve today's problems but ensure its long-term survival – because it won't become obsolete. This is good for owners and shareholders, and it's also good for employees who futureproof their job skills at the same time.

The methodology will do more than make your company run better. It will help you rediscover the joy of building, the joy of tinkering, the joy of playing and experimenting. It'll help you fall in love with your business and the work you do.

I sometimes get resistance to operationalizing. There's a fear, especially by right-brained thinkers, that it will rob the owners and team of the creative joy of building. Look, you've chosen to read a book on making your business better. If everything were roses you wouldn't be here.

**The fact is, constraints breed creativity.** By putting in place a simple architecture it frees you to be creative where it counts. You'll have more energy, and more excitement because it's all directed – instead of diffused.

# How to Read This Book

In this section, I'll go over how to use this book so you can get the most from it in the least amount of time.

Most importantly, give yourself permission to *not* read this book cover to cover. Depending on your goals, and what kind of material sticks with you the most, you might be better off skipping around to get the most value.

Here's how to use this book:

- Step 1: think about why this book applies to your situation. You'll get 10x the amount out of it if you do. Do this by reading this introduction to understand why it's important, then write down how it applies to your goals here. Why is this important to you?

  _____

  _____

  _____

- Step 2: some people hate business stories – and others find they help cement ideas and make them real.
  - If stories help you understand information better, and you want to fully internalize the frameworks in this book, read Part One straight through.

- ○ If you're just looking for the big picture (possibly at the expense of not internalizing it as much) go through Part One reading the "just the facts" material in the gray boxes.
- ○ Make sure to visit TheBusinessUnlock.com/resources to download the electronic copies of the explanatory notes so you have them handy in the future.
- Step 3: If you are ready to get started implementing in your business now, read Part Two. If not, skip it until you want to put it into practice – there's no reason to fill your brain with that until you want to take action.
- Step 4: If you are interested in future-proofing your business so you don't fall behind the competition, read Part Three.

The companion website at TheBusinessUnlock.com/resources will also give you access to worksheets as well as companion materials not available in the book, so make sure you visit there.

In fact, do it now while you're thinking about it.

# PART ONE

# THE FRAMEWORK

# Inputs, Process, Output

Ryan knew he wasn't being a good father at that moment, but couldn't help it.

He was supposed to be playing Legos with Jack, but The Rustic Oven was failing – and his mind was on how few customers had ordered his gourmet pizzas that week.

Jack had said something. Ryan dragged himself back to the present.

"Huh?"

"The instructions say we build the landing gear next"

"Sounds good kiddo."

Ryan thought about increasing his Google ads budget. Or should he do another mailer? Or maybe...

"Dad"

… Dino's Pizza down the road was doing coupons on Facebook, and he hadn't tried that. No, his place was high-end, coupons would damage the brand. But what would…

"DAD"

"Yeah sorry I'm paying attention," he lied.

"The landing gear gets put together before the main hold, help me find these pieces," he said, pointing to the instructions for the parts bags he had just dumped out.

"On it. Let's see if we can't finish the landing gear before we have to head to the airport"

Ryan hadn't done Legos since he was twelve, and had bought the Millennium Falcon kit on impulse for Jack. Right now, searching for parts was strangely satisfying. He had an instruction manual and had to just do what it said and would get the result they wanted.

But his always-on business brain had registered something about building.

"If only The Rustic Oven were as simple. Wait … It is!"

He found another couple of pieces, gave them to Jack, and grabbed the pen near him on the table. Taking a paper napkin from the stack, he scrawled a diagram on it:

The Lego set was just that – a set of *inputs*, a *process* for assembling them into something else, and an end *output*.

He wasn't sure why, but that had something to do with The Rustic Oven.

"Can I take the set with me to Thanksgiving? It gets so boring with all the grownup talk and I want something to do" asked Jack.

"As long as you're responsible for the pieces not getting lost, I'm sure Mom won't mind."

"Deal!"

The phone rang, and Ryan's heart sank when he saw the number. It was his restaurant supplier, and he was 30 days past due on the bill.

Ryan hoped for the best and picked up.

"Hey Phil"

"Bad news Ryan," came the voice on the other end. Ryan steeled himself.

"Oh?"

"Yeah, the fontina you always get isn't available. Might be a two-week delay. Want to replace it with something else? Gruyère?"

"Nope, I can't make *Fontina Iron Kiss* without fontina. I'll just leave it off the menu for the next couple of weeks. Thanks for letting me know–" hanging up before Phil looked into his account balance.

That was it. It was like the Legos.

Dough, fontina, onions, olive oil, garlic and balsamic were *inputs*. Baking was the *process*. Pizza was the *output*.

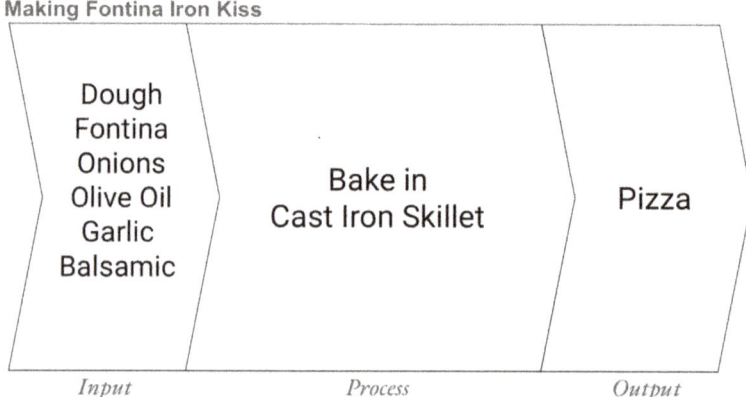

Making Fontina Iron Kiss

Dough
Fontina
Onions
Olive Oil
Garlic
Balsamic

Bake in
Cast Iron Skillet

Pizza

*Input*          *Process*          *Output*

"Thirty minutes, Jackster. Pack up the set-" called Mom from the other room.

It was almost time to head to the airport. Ryan stuffed the napkin in his pocket and went to collect the bags.

> Every business is made up of *processes* that have *inputs* and *outputs*

# Subprocesses

There were dozens of people at Thanksgiving, but that's how his in-laws always did it. The more, the merrier. He'd be fine as long as he didn't get assigned a seat next to Melvin … and have to hear (again) about how nobody had bought the old man's screenplay for 30 years. He could always make an excuse that Jack needed company and leave the table.

Ryan sat with Jack in the living room, absentmindedly watching the boy attach the cockpit subassembly to the body of the Falcon.

*Inputs → Process → Output*

There it was, again. But now he saw the inputs weren't the individual bricks. They were the subassemblies Jack had made earlier. Landing gear, cockpit … each a component of the whole.

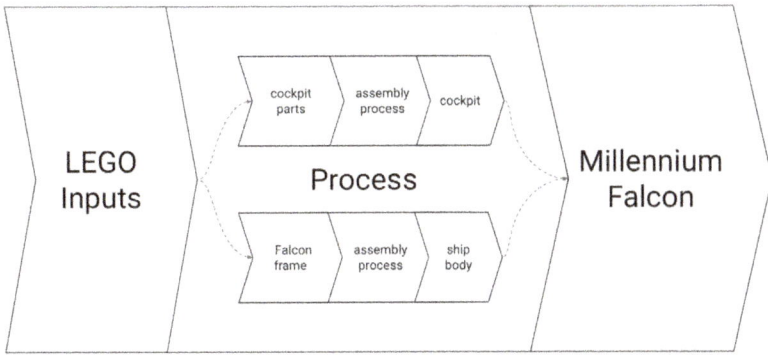

Of course. Making a pizza had subprocesses too. Ryan pulled out the napkin again.

Baking wasn't just one thing. Checking the temperature, rotating the pie, making sure it was at the right spot in the wood-fired oven, and making sure the timing was right.

The baking step had sub-processes.

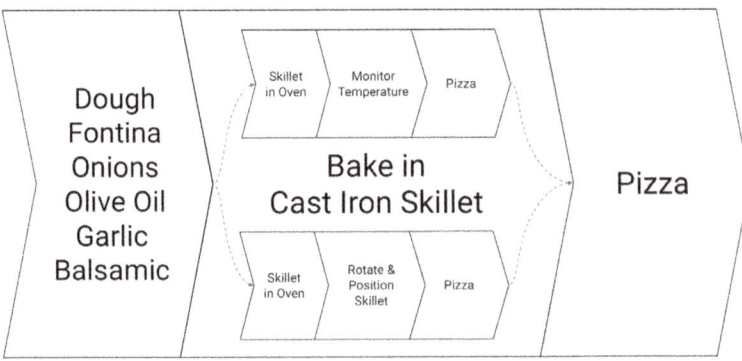

And it wasn't just making the pizza. Before that, he had to market to get customers. After he had to deliver it. And each of those had subprocesses.

His weren't written down like the Lego instructions, but he definitely did the same thing each time. And each time he had to teach a new employee how to do it from scratch…

He heard his father-in-law holler from the dining room. Time for dinner.

He'd better not be stuck next to Melvin.

---

Every process can be made up of other processes

# Pipelining – Putting Processes Together

Ryan's seat was near the end of the second table, and as he sat down he tossed the diagrammed napkin on the table, then glanced over at the place card next to his.

On one side, his better half was already chatting away with the rest of the table.

On the other side his second cousin Alex, he noted with relief. About five or six years older, and worked at Apple. Alex was quiet, and that worked out well for him because his job was some hush-hush secret thing making new products.

"Hey," said Alex, sitting down, "Jack here?"

"Yeah, he's playing in the living room. He'll eat over there."

And, like every time with Alex, there was an awkwardly long pause.

"What's that?" asked Alex after a pause.

"What's what?"

"The napkin. Something for the restaurant?"

"Sort of. I was watching Jack play with Legos and I just saw there was a framework to the whole thing. And it applied to my business as well. I thought it was interesting."

"Tell me about it," said Alex, seeming genuinely interested in a conversation with Ryan for the first time.

Ryan unfolded the napkin and took Alex through his realizations about *inputs → process → output,* and how the model could be nested for bigger and smaller processes.

And – as he now realized – even an entire business is *inputs → process → output.*

Alex stared at the napkin.

"Actually, you're on to something here. At Apple our manufacturing is the same thing. Obviously, we have components → assembly → phone. The components of the phone get assembled into a phone. But these aren't just nested. They're pipelined as well."

"Pipelined?" asked Ryan

"Yeah, once a phone comes out of assembly, it needs to go into the packaging, and that gets put together, then shipped to a warehouse. So think of it like there are two inputs, the phone and the box, each with its own inputs and outputs. And those outputs, the phone and the box, aren't sold – they're *outputs* of that process – and *inputs* to the packaging process that comes next. That process outputs a phone in a box, ready to be shipped. Can I borrow your pen?"

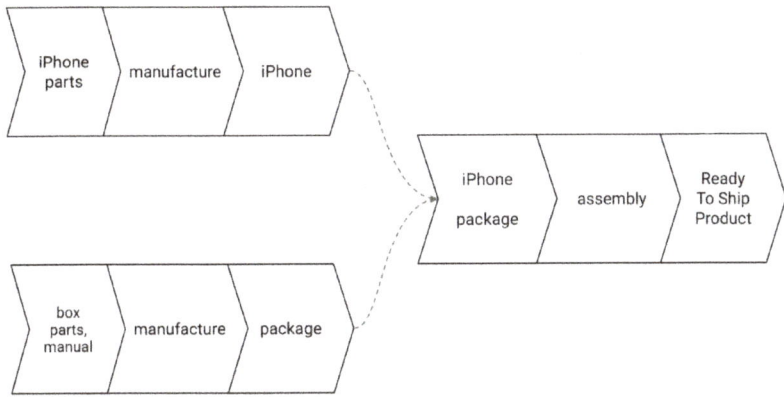

"That makes a lot of sense," said Ryan "I've got the same thing for my delivery kid Kyle – but he gets the "outputs" he needs from different steps.

He takes the address from the order, and the pizza that was made from the order, and those two things are what he needs to deliver to the customer.

The first napkin had run out of space, so Ryan grabbed three more sensing there would be more sketching ahead of them.

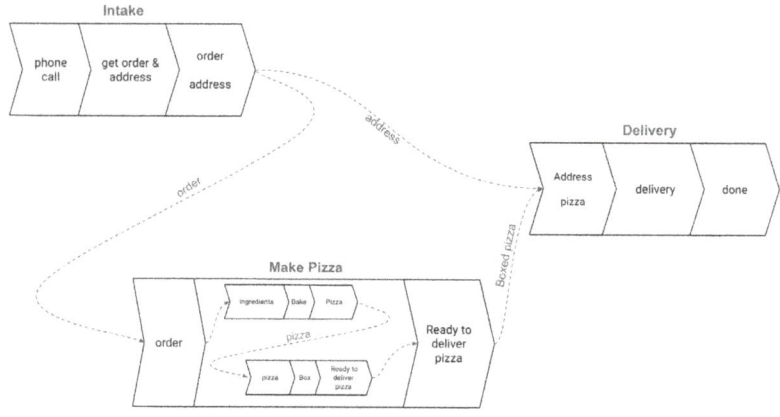

*The Rustic Oven order-taking, pizza-baking, and delivery process*

"I think we're onto something that works for any business," mused Alex.

Ryan thought for a moment.

"This is great … but business doesn't always run like clockwork. I know, I run a dysfunctional business." said Ryan. "What about when something goes wrong?"

> Outputs of one process can be inputs to another.
> Lining these up is key to understanding the system as a whole.

## 1.4

# Exceptions – When Things Break

"Anticipating problems is a big part of what I need to do at Apple," said Alex, "I can only talk about the things already in the news – but you'll remember that we had disruptions at our Foxconn facility during COVID."

"Yeah, I remember that. I wanted the new iPhone 14 and couldn't get one"

"Well, our plans made the disruptions a lot less painful than they could have been."

"Wait," said Ryan, "what if that's part of the framework?"

"What do you mean?"

"This business framework. We've got *inputs* coming in, and *outputs* going out. But when something goes wrong – an exception from the norm – the process could deal with that" pondered Ryan.

"We should have the model include what an *exception* is, and what do do," added Alex

"OK let's keep this simple for my pizza shop. Last week Kyle was delivering, and the address was an apartment building and he didn't have an apartment number. He called the number on the order, but nobody was answering the phone. He just went knocking on doors. But that wasn't a great idea because someone could have said the order was theirs. Not to mention he was out for an extra 20 minutes and other orders started piling up."

"So how would you handle it?" asked Alex

"If it were me, if he couldn't find the destination, and they don't pick up the phone, I'd have him move on to the next order, putting this one at the back of the line, then try calling again at the end. No reason for all the other customers who gave good information to get cold pizza. Like this – "

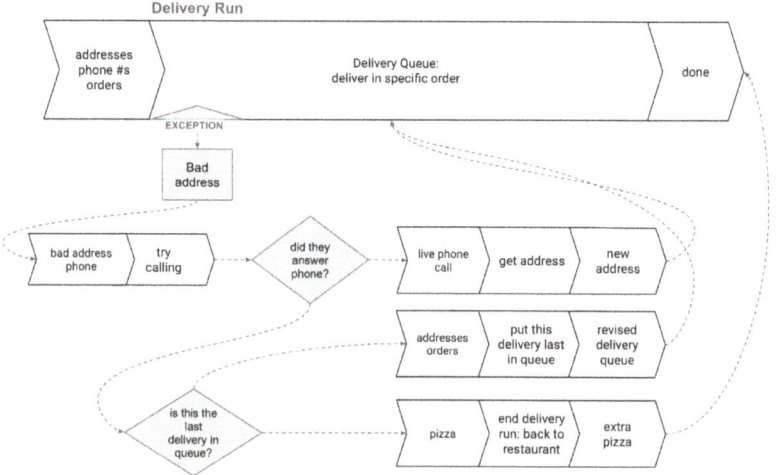

*The Rustic Oven delivery run process*

"It feels complicated," said Ryan, "it's such a simple process but now there are all these arrows –"

Alex interrupted him "I worked in a small startup before joining Apple. And one thing I'm sure of – I was on call 24x7 because they didn't get detailed. Besides, when you boil it down it's the same pattern repeating again and again … so it's still pretty simple now that we have the basics down."

"Actually, that's true, I documented some parts of the business. Like if one of the employees is sick, they know who to call to open up the shop in the morning. And it made my life way easier. I just didn't realize until now that *every* process needs a list of exceptions."

Alex added, "Right – at Apple we focus a lot on 'contingency planning' … but for this framework, if we add exceptions to each process it's a much simpler way of thinking about it."

The cousins had barely touched their meal and saw others getting up to trade in their plates for pie.

"OK," said Ryan, shoveling down the last bits of turkey as he thought out loud, "All of this makes sense in the physical world. But if we're on to a truly universal business framework then it needs to work for everything."

"So what's a hard case," said Alex, rising to get his pie before it was all gone.

"How about marketing?"

"Ooh. Good one. Get your pie and let's figure that one out."

> Things will go wrong. Documenting *exceptions* and what to do when that happens is key to giving the business owner freedom and the business enterprise value.

# 1.5

# Logs – Finding Problems
# & Optimizing Processes

"So marketing," said Alex plopping himself into the chair.

"Marketing. Pizza marketing isn't the most sophisticated. How do you think about that at Apple?"

"Usual disclaimers, I can't say if anything does or doesn't happen at Apple, confidentiality and all…"

"Right, right" said Ryan with an exaggerated eye roll.

"We go through something similar to most big companies I've worked with. We've got an insanely valuable brand, so any marketing has to be completely aligned with that. Usually I'm involved with campaigns for a new product launch, so the internal team decides on what success looks like. Then an agency and our internal team work on creatives and audiences. Then we launch a campaign, and try to tie the customer acquisition numbers to the campaign."

"OK, well the model works," said Ryan.

"Tell me."

"For your marketing initiative, the inputs are brand, creatives and offer. The process is creating success criteria, launching the campaign, and measuring it by logging performance. And the output is customers. Of course, you can have subprocesses for each of these like we talked about."

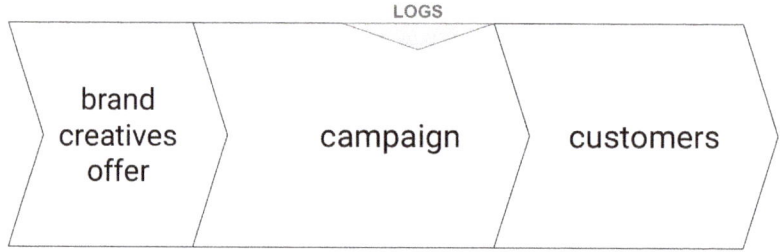

"Of course," said Alex.

"Actually, that's not so different from what I do, now that we've simplified it. I'm running more direct response ads to get people to come into the store instead of product awareness ads. But there's one thing I'm not doing."

"What's that"

"Measuring. I mean I kind of have a general idea of what's working. I hope. Or maybe I don't."

"Let's work through it." Said Alex helpfully.

"I'm running two kinds of campaigns. I'm running Google ads online, and also doing mailers to a one-mile radius of the shop."

Ryan continued, "I know that when I spend more, more customers come in, but I haven't been tracking if one is more effective than the other."

"So you could be increasing the budget for both when one is more effective," said Alex, taking the pen. "So you should really treat each one as a separate subprocess so you can track it. Kind of like this – "

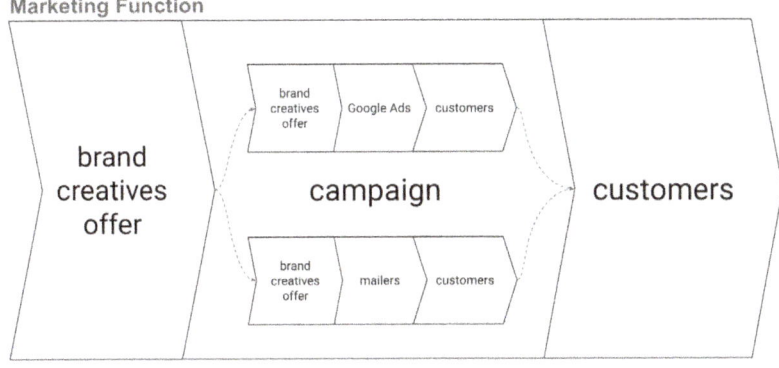

"Bingo," said Alex, "you need to log that information"

"So *logs*. That's the other thing" said Ryan. "We have *inputs, processes, outputs* and *exceptions*. But the key to improving any process is logs. Tracking what's happening <u>inside</u> the process, so you can make the process better."

"Exactly." continued Alex. "So for your shop, log each campaign and you'll see which is performing better. Then you can change the mix. And it might change over time, like you might get more results from mailers at the beginning of the school year or something – but tracking it within the process is how you'll know that."

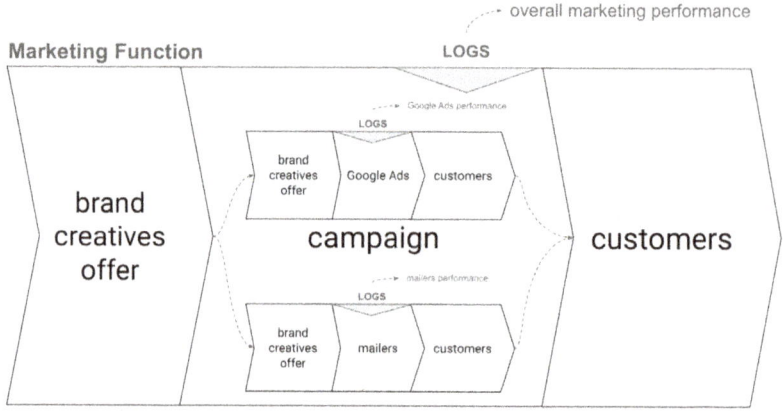

"I think we just fixed my customer problem," smiled Ryan.

"Hey – this has been great – but I'm half an hour late for hitting the road. Off to New York on a late flight. When are you headed back?" Alex wasn't in the least bit awkward anymore.

"Tomorrow," said Ryan, "and I should really check on Jack. He's probably finished the Falcon by now."

> *Logs* let you track what's working, what's not working, and are the key to making the business better over time

# Futureproofing the Business

At the airport the next morning the flight was delayed – it was fortunate Jack wasn't quite done with the Lego set. Ryan's wife went to find food for the family, and Jack spread out what remained of the kit – mostly engine detailing – on the floor.

Ryan sat down nearby and pulled out a notebook and uncrumpled the napkin, copying down the diagrams and jotting down notes so he could think more about them.

Another boy about Jack's age asked if he could help with the legos. Jack looked at him for a second suspiciously, looked away, then said "Sure."

"That your boy?" asked a scruffy man in a hoodie sitting across from Ryan.

"Yes," said Ryan, half wondering if he was dealing with a creep – or just a curious type.

"The one that just butted into his Lego building is mine. Sorry about that. I'm David."

"Ryan"

"Drawing something? Artist?" asked David, then paused. "Sorry, now I'm butting in. Like father, like son."

Ryan was a little irritated, but at least the guy was self-aware. Maybe he was just a talker – he gave him a pass.

"No, just copying down some notes. I had a chat with my cousin at Thanksgiving and it's given me a lot to think about for running my business."

"What kind of business?"

"Pizza place"

"Ad agency," David said, leaning forward and pointing at himself.

"Really? I talked a bunch about ad campaigns last night as well."

"What about?"

"Well, we realized that we could boil down every process both in Apple and a pizza parlor, including marketing and advertising, into a framework. It kind of atomizes the business into components"

Ryan held up the sketches.

"Pretty neat, mind if I take a closer look?"

"Sure"

David crossed over and sat next to Ryan, who gave him a rundown of how the framework worked.

"You know," said David after absorbing it, "I never thought about it that way – but some of the stuff I'm doing with automating my agency would fit perfectly with this."

"Really?" said Ryan, intrigued, "tell me more."

"Our agency works with Fortune 500 companies, helping them localize their ad campaigns. For example, a big brand like Nike has campaigns in the USA – but they can't run the same ads all over the world. Obviously, the languages are different – but also the models pictured need to be relevant to a target audience … But they can't be totally different. Those changes need to be made in a way that still is within brand guidelines. We help companies take their ad campaigns global."

"OK, I get it. But what's this about automation?" asked Ryan.

"That's what fits perfectly with your framework. Each campaign is a series of *inputs* – the original USA campaign, the brand guidelines, the offer – as well as one more thing, which is where it's being localized for and the target audience. Then we have a process to localize the campaign, and the output is a new campaign for that market."

"So to use the Nike example," he continued, "the ad being localized for India would have the model wearing the shoes look like Indian athletes, not American or Chinese ones. And our special sauce is that our process is done by AI, with the help of some humans. Since AI got so good at imagery it lets us do things we could never do before. Before, we were hiring photo models in each region and re-doing the photoshoots."

David described their process at a high level, as Ryan sketched it:

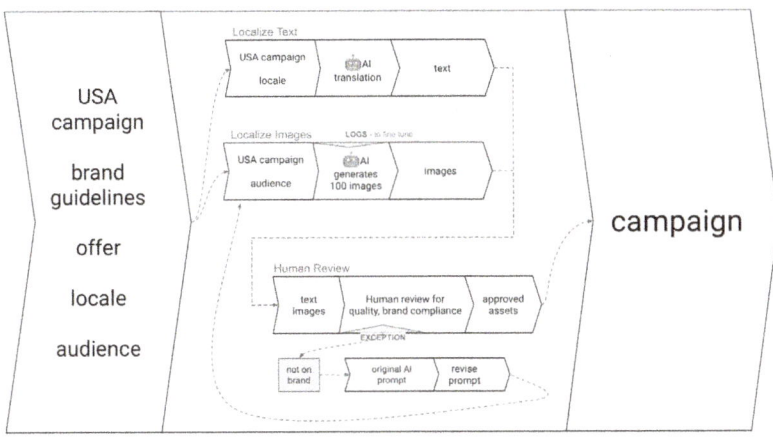

"So," asked Ryan, "because you've defined the process you can take something that was done expensively by people, and use AI to do it faster and cheaper?"

"Exactly. Obviously, we have people in the mix, both for helping define the inputs and approve the outputs, as you call them. But we replaced a human process with an AI process."

"And," said Ryan, feeling clever, "if you atomize your whole business into this framework, you can find other ways to use AI."

"Right! It's not all-or-nothing. We've only done this for the creatives so far. But once the business is broken down using your framework, we can decide when new technologies are good enough, and swap just the pieces that are ready. We'll be able to stay ahead of everyone because we'll be looking at it in discrete units."

"And – since you've got the logs, you can track employee hours and effort … you'll be able to see where things are inefficient to look for opportunities –"

"Finished!" yelled Jack, running up to the two men, who were both lost in thought.

# PART TWO

# IMPLEMENTING THE BUSINESS UNLOCK SYSTEM

This section is the instruction manual. If you've jumped here without reading Part One, you can get started right away.

If you've just read the story in Part One, don't skip this part. I know, it's not as 'fun' as a story for some, but this is where the rubber meets the road for your own business.

Before we jump in, let's make sure you are going to get the most out of this part. Answer these questions so your brain will be actively involved in your business, not passively "reading stuff."

1.  What Big Problem are you dealing with in your business right now that you're unsure how to solve?

    _____

    _____

    _____

2.  What Big Opportunity do you want to capitalize on in your business that you're unsure how to start on?

    _____

    _____

    _____

We're going to address your Big Problem, and let you capitalize on your Big Opportunity with the three Business Unlock principles:

- Every business is made up of *processes* that have *inputs* and *outputs*.
- Every process can be made up of other processes.
- If you atomize your business this way, you can easily diagnose *problems* and unlock *possibilities*.

This Part Two will explain each of these principles, explain why it's essential, and give you examples of how to apply it. But first, let's make this more real with an example.

Joe runs a software startup that he's been grinding on for two years. The software is on the market, but almost nobody is buying. He reads this book (because he's smart), and fills in the questions as follows:

1. What Big Problem are you dealing with in your business right now that you're unsure how to solve?

   When we get customers, we keep them for a long time. The problem is we're not getting many. Nobody is finding out about us. I'm tweeting and posting in forums, and tried paid ads, but nothing seems to work.

2. What Big Opportunity do you want to capitalize on in your business that you're unsure how to start on?

*Since our software takes some set-up, we do a bunch of services during the first 90 days. If we could partner with consultants to do the services component we could focus more on the software and our margins would improve drastically.*

How are the Business Unlock principles going to help Joe?

- Every business is made up of *processes* that have *inputs* and *outputs*.

  We break down the processes Joe is using to acquire customers to see what's working, what's not working, and what could be changed to meet the goal of more customers. For his Big Opportunity, we work backward from what output he wants (an effective partnership program), see what process gets him there, and then what inputs are needed.

- Every process can be made up of other processes.

  Both his problem and opportunity are not one step. They'll take multiple components (sub-processes), so we disassemble them to define each of those so we know how the machine works before we run off implementing.

Now you have an idea of how both your Big Problem and Big Opportunity could be tackled. But before we do that, I want to introduce you to someone.

His name is Rogue Robot. After this book, when he's helped you fix problems in your business and uncover opportunities you never knew existed, he may be your best friend. I'll be a little jealous since you'll like him more than me, but I'll get over it because you visited TheBusinessUnlock.com/resources and watched the bonus videos there and Rogue Robot can't make videos as good as mine.

Since you've just met Rogue Robot, let me introduce him:

1. He's a robot (he could be an A.I. like ChatGPT, an automation platform like Zapier, or any other software). Being a robot, if you tell him to do something he'll do it. You love him for this. He can make your life so much easier.
2. He's a rascal, so if you aren't *painfully* explicit in giving him what he needs, he'll just make shit up. The worst part is what he makes up will usually be something that produces a bad result that embarrasses you, and he'll laugh at you in a tinny voice and you'll be so fucking pissed.

You're about to hire Rogue Robot.

**Why Standard Operating Procedures Aren't Enough**

When business owners try to make their businesses more efficient or effective, they often put together Standard Operating Procedures (SOPs). And when you're putting together SOPs, you're usually thinking "How might someone screw this up." The same way McDonald's can get millions of teens with 20-second TikTok attention spans to make consistent burgers across the globe.

Realize it or not, a successful SOP is written for a Rogue Robot. This is because he does exactly what you say to do, and you're trying to be super explicit so he doesn't screw up and put the mustard on TOP of the bun – because that would suck, and he'll do it to embarrass you, trust me.

There are two problems with SOPs:

1. They are preventative, not diagnostic. When you first make them you'll decrease errors, but then they are static. Your employees are being told what to do, but it isn't helping to fix ongoing problems or spot opportunities.
2. They aren't nested, meaning they are only at one level, and not connecting to each other. This means they don't give a true systems-level view of the business.

The way most businesses implement SOPs is usually a linear checklist of "things to do" (do this, then do this, …). Which is great: those things get done, steps don't get missed, and uncertainty goes down. But – and it's a big but – SOPs usually don't help with driving a company forward: finding problems and possibilities. It's a snapshot in time. We might call them Stupidly Outdated Policies.

We're looking to do more than create a static checklist of things to do. If we've learned anything in the past decade, it's that business is evolving fast. Static checklists could last for ages when Miami Vice was on primetime[2], but now – not so much.

**Processes Within Processes**

The other problem is SOPs aren't *nested*. That is, they're a list of things on one level. But, a business isn't a one-level thing. It's got functions (marketing, finance, delivery), and each of those has pieces (advertising, content creation, lead capture), and each of those has pieces, and so on. Most SOPs address their own little universe and don't connect with other checklists. That means most SOPs are not part of a whole *system*.

For the Business Unlock individual processes themselves are only a part of the picture. In other words, this is bigger than SOPs. It's about how processes are *linked to* each other.

You're in one of two places right now:

| If you haven't done an SOP in your company yet: that's fine because the process we'll go through here is higher-level, and will help you develop solid SOPs later. | If you have done SOPs already: you'll get to leverage the groundwork you did there and get a far bigger impact with the work you've already done. |
|---|---|

---

2   Look, I told you if you didn't want 80's references this wasn't the book for you.

# Every Business Is Made of Processes

If you feel like your company is a tangled mess, you're never really on top of what's happening, and you're just waiting for something to break, it's because you haven't broken it down into processes.

The first thing is to recognize that *every single thing that happens in your business is a process.* Younger me would have looked for reasons this isn't true – "What about X" – and yammer on about creativity, relationships, or something else. Younger me was wrong.

The first step: if you have any resistance to the idea that every single thing in your business is a process, it's time to drop it now. Suspend disbelief and just play along if you have to.

A process requires three things:

- The *inputs* to the process. That is, the inputs into the process
- The *process* itself (if you have SOPs, this is where they live)
- The *outputs* of the process

We diagram it as follows:

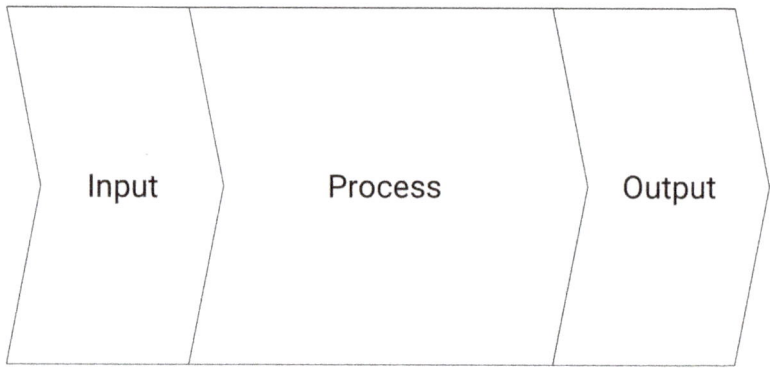

Before getting to examples, let's look at each of those things with the help of Rogue Robot. We're going to engineer every process in your business to be run by Rogue Robot.

## Explanation of Inputs

*Inputs* are "anything that is required to do the process." So if a process needs some piece of information, access to something, or a physical object, it's an *input*.

Since there can be multiple inputs needed, note that those inputs can be coming from *other* processes – maybe even multiple other processes. That's how these will link together.

We need to be super explicit about inputs because if we aren't then Rogue Robot gets to make shit up.

For example, you've got a marketing agency, and Rogue Robot is great at making social media posts, but you forgot to give him access to the password. So, because it will be hilarious for him and painful for you, he decides to do 10 password attempts and lock you out of the account. Fucking hate that guy.

So the bottom line is, your inputs list must be painfully accurate.

In fact, let's do this: we're locking Rogue Robot in his room and he can't come out. Everything he needs to do a process must be fed to him through a food slot in the door. This will help us later when we get to diagnosing problems.

## Explanation of Process

*Process* is the step-by-step of what happens to complete the thing that's being done.

This can be checklist-like, but it can also have "branches" in it. For example, do Step 1, then if the result of Step 1 is the customer ordered a hamburger, then Step 2 is 'pack a hamburger' – but if they ordered a chicken sandwich, then Step 2 is 'pack a chicken sandwich.'

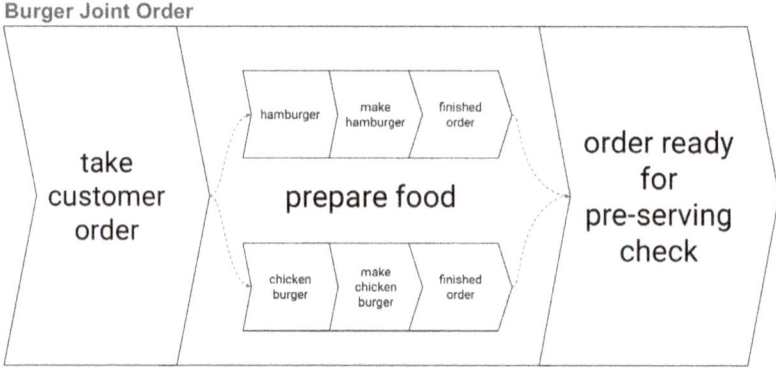

*Simplified order-taking at the burger joint*

Again, we need to be very explicit, because you hired Rogue Robot. If we are not VERY clear, all our hamburgers are getting the condiments on top of the bun. And then the milkshake is poured on top of the contents of the bag instead of in a cup.

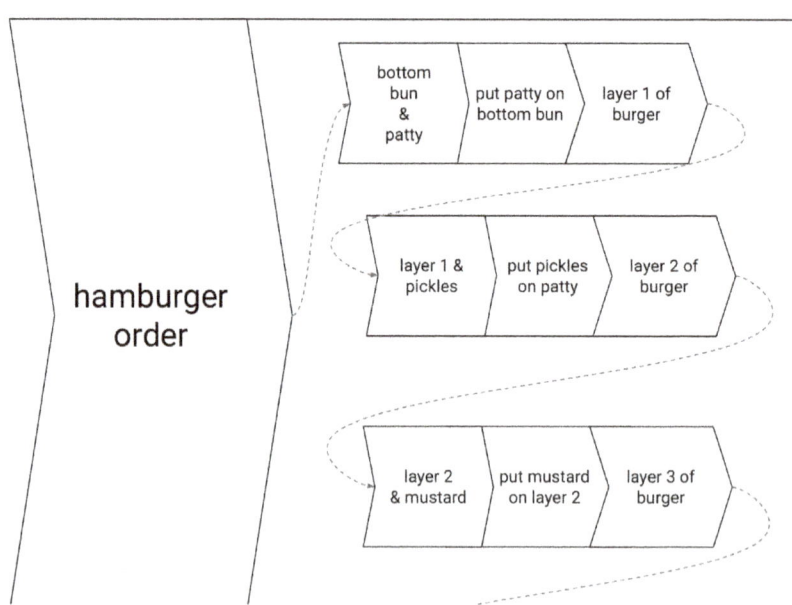

*Partial diagram of assembling a burger*

## Explanation of Output

*Output* is "whatever comes out of this process." Sometimes this is obvious, like in manufacturing where the output is a product. But sometimes it's less obvious, for example where you have a sales process and out of it comes both customers as well as signed contracts. As alluded to above, this is because the outputs here can be inputs somewhere else – the customers go into the onboarding process, and the contracts into the filing documents process.

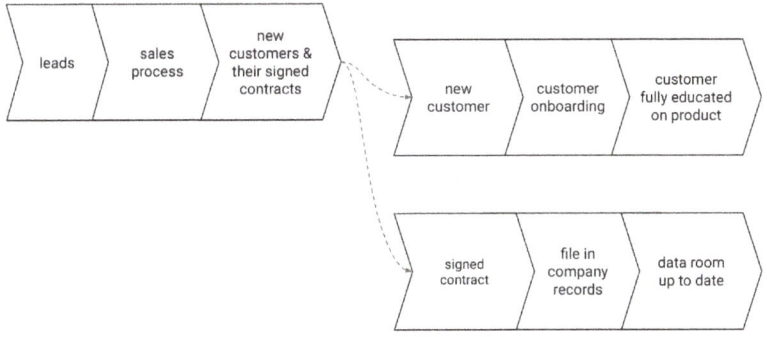

Do we have to be explicit about what the output looks like here? Well, just imagine what Rogue Robot is going to do if you aren't. Those contracts will all be in Sanskrit, because that'll be funny when you go to sell the company and it fucks up your diligence.

## Examples

Now that you understand the three components of a process, here are some examples. They're intentionally simple because I don't know if your business is software or chicken rentals[3], so tweak them for your situation.

Marketing is a process:

> brand, creatives, offer → campaigns → leads

Selling expensive things is a process

> leads → sales conversation → customers

Selling cheap things on the Internet is a process

> leads → order form → customers

Selling things in retail stores is a process

> Store buyer relationships → fulfillment of inventory → invoices

Selling high-touch, face-to-face personal services is a process

> relationships → weekly golf course outings → customers

Customer service is a process

> customer inquiry → case resolution → happy customer

---

3   Yes, this is real. https://link.rajjha.com/rent-chickens

## Let's Make It Real For You

Remember I asked you to write down a Big Problem at the beginning of Part Two? Let's start fixing it.

If you haven't downloaded the worksheets at TheBusinessUnlock. com/resources now is the time to do it.

We're going to start with a high-level diagram.

1.  Identify the part of the business that's causing you trouble, and identify the process that covers this part of the business. For example, it could be "I'm not getting enough leads" – so the process we're working on is "lead generation." Or, it might be "my subscription customers aren't staying long enough" in which case the process is "customer retention."

2.  Use the diagram format *inputs* → *process* → *output* and write out in detail:

    a.  All the *inputs* that are, or should, be going into the process,

    b.  The *process* itself. At this point, it can be high level. For example, you can just say "send emails" instead of detailing every step of how to send emails. As you write it out, you'll likely start to see where the Big Problem is manifesting itself in the process.

    c.  The *output* that comes out and might feed into other processes.

Below is a blank one for you. It's a bit small, so you can also download free worksheets as fillable PDFs or use a free online tool at <u>TheBusinessUnlock.com/resources</u>.

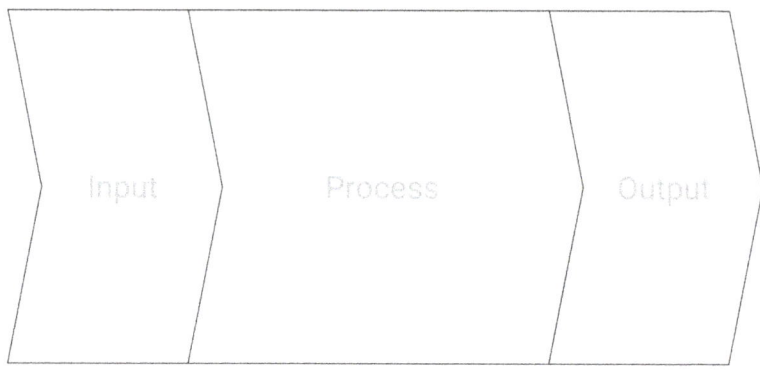

3. Then, do the following, adjusting the diagram based on your answers:

   a. What in my diagram is missing in the business? For example, do I have a process where some information isn't always readily available and would improve completing the process?

   b. If I gave my diagram to Rogue Robot to run, how would he try to humiliate me?

   c. Circle areas in the diagram which would have the biggest impact on your Big Problem.

## 2.2

# Any Process Can Contain Other Processes

Every business *itself* is a process. It takes in capital and resources, does some "stuff", and out comes products/services, and (hopefully a lot of) profit:

capital, resources → business → products/services, profit

We all know a business has several functions in it, such as marketing, sales, customer service, finance, and delivery. We saw that each one of those functions can be diagrammed as a process. So each of those functions fits within the Business Unlock framework.

We know that processes can be *nested* (processes within processes) using the same Business Unlock diagramming framework. This is an important concept because it allows us to "zoom in" to the right level of the organization to fix something or find opportunities.

Let's take the example of a marketing department tasked with generating leads for sales.

budget → marketing → leads

When I was starting an eCommerce business, I kept it simple. I had a budget to test marketing messages with the output being leads. I chose Facebook to run my tests and would count up the leads generated by each test. So each *month* my process looked like this:

test budget → four test campaigns on Facebook → leads

We'll learn more about measuring performance later. At this point, we're just understanding that a process is a thing you'll repeat on some frequency and get a result.

## Nested Processes

We know that the marketing function has a lot of sub-steps in it. When I was running a marketing agency, we did a lot of blog writing for clients and also managed their paid ads. Let's say a client was just publishing blog articles for SEO and running Facebook ads. That means the "marketing" process might be comprised of three processes, that run at different times:

do once and repeat every 3 years:

existing brand → brand development → revised brand

Repeat daily:

brand, ideal customer → SEO → blog article

Repeat Ongoing:

brand, budget → Facebook ads → leads

And of course, we could dig down to further levels if we wanted. For example, the SEO process could be comprised of

Repeat monthly:

customer research → keyword analysis → keywords, topics

Daily:

Keywords, topics → article research → research brief

Research brief, keywords → write blog article → blog article, keywords

Blog article, keywords → publish to blog → live URL

Live URL → publish to social media → live URLs

Of course, there are an infinite number of ways you can break things down. I can't give you the "one way to do it" because each business is different, and the flexibility in how you break down processes is what gives power when you start diagnosing problems and finding opportunities. However, if you are running any kind of process for a client, it does help to standardize so you can take learnings from one client to the next.

One common question is, "How granular should I make my

diagram?" At some point, it becomes ridiculous when you're being completely obvious. In most cases, you'll want to document down to this level:

a) Anything where Rogue Robot could screw up and totally embarrass you or screw up your business, and

b) Areas where things are going wrong in your business should get the microscope so you can diagnose the issue. You might not use that level of detail for your company playbook, but for diagnostic purposes, it can be invaluable.

Rogue Robot might screw up something minor, like putting a file in the wrong folder. Embarrassing? Probably not. Screw up the company totally? Unlikely. So at this point, you would leave it off the diagram.

However, if the process is writing an article, a plagiarism check might be a good idea. Because if you have a rogue writer like I did at my agency, it can become a company-compromising event. Clients leaving, reputation impacted, and potential lawsuits. That was not fun.

Now that you know how to divide things up into pieces, let's use the next principle to help diagnose your Big Problem.

# 2.3

# Diagnosing Problems

You have the business diagrammed, now how do you figure out what's wrong, and how to fix it? Pull out the diagram you created in the last chapter.

You circled areas in the diagram that will have the biggest impact on the Big Problem.

For each of those areas, "zoom in" by documenting (or creating) subprocesses. What we're doing is trying to pull apart the Big Problem into sub-pieces to identify where the problem lies.

Sometimes, you'll find you *thought* the problem was one thing, but in actuality, it's just a small subset of it. For example, you thought customer acquisition was broken, but it's just that the sales reps aren't following up to get contracts signed. They get a verbal "yes" and collect payment – but forget to get the signed agreement.

Sometimes, diagramming the business and teasing apart the problem parts will give you a "no WONDER this is happening" moment.

But what if it doesn't?

## Tricky Dependencies

Sometimes we need to dig deeper because a problem is more complicated. You've teased apart the Big Problem area and it's still not obvious what the solution is.

Often this happens when there's a *dependency* you're not seeing. You're looking at your diagram and the system appears fine at first glance … but two or more pieces (which might not be right next to each other) aren't playing well together.

A few years ago this bit me in the butt. Sales performance was starting to go down at one of my companies. The sales reps had good close rates – the close percentages hadn't changed. That couldn't be the problem. Our lead generation was doing *better* than it had a year ago – so more leads were coming in. Prices had gone *up*. But our total new revenue was going *down*. Why, if our lead generation was improving, and our prices were up, was revenue not improving?

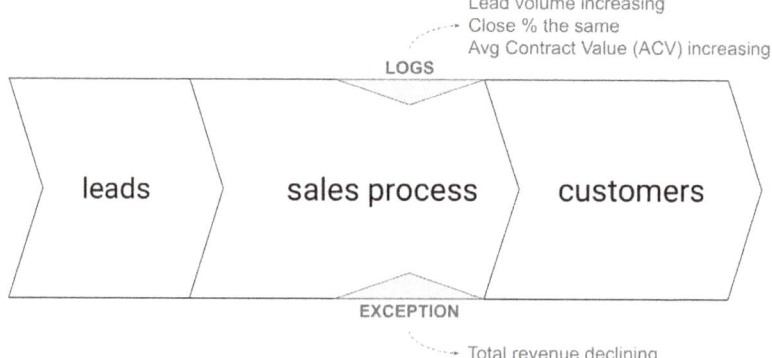

I teased apart the sales process function and nothing lept off the page. I was scratching my head. I had to drop a log on my head.

## Drop a Log On Your Head

Up until now, we've talked about your business diagram as something static. You have a process, you run the process. Kind of like a souped-up SOP (that is, Stupidly Outdated Policies).

That's why I didn't see where things were going wrong with my sales department.

The trick to diagnosing dependency problems is (drumroll please) *tracking the right things.*

I was tracking the number of leads, and I could see they were going up. I was tracking revenue, and that was going down. So I peeked into sales close percentages, and those were steady.

In other words, I was looking at the things most business owners look at: numbers and percentages at each link in the chain.

But here's where we have to start viewing your business not just as a series of processes that are one and done, but *through time.*

There was an increase in output from the Leads process: I'd replaced my original lead process with a new one, and more leads were exiting that process, and entering the sales process.

I had measured my close rates on the sales process: for a given number of leads getting to that process, the same number were getting through.

What I hadn't measured: was *how long* between when a lead came in and when they got to the sales appointment.

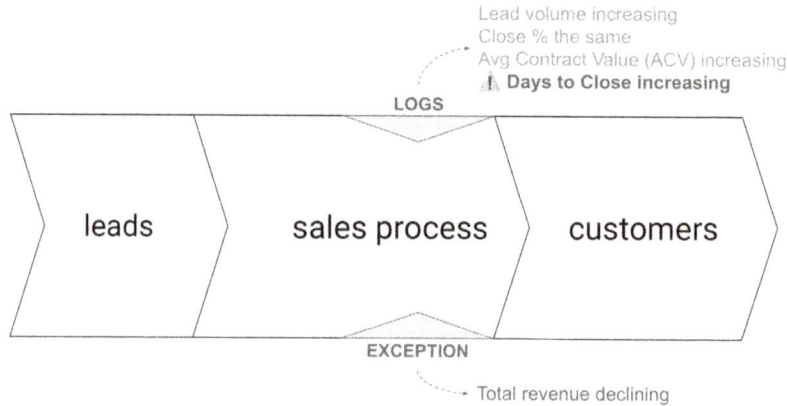

Oh shit. Scramble to figure that out. Don't have the data. Spend weeks collecting data…

Turns out, that we were getting way more leads interested in the concept – but that wasn't translating to people interested in a call. In fact, on average it was taking almost *twice* as long to get from lead to sales. Leads were taking more convincing through our marketing before closing.

The reps hadn't been screaming for lack of lead flow because we'd started a new campaign to existing leads which had covered up the problem (until we ran through our backlog of leads).

Using the analogy of the Water Works plumbing game from my childhood, I'd replaced my short sales pipe with one that let in more leads (water), but it snaked around and was twice as long. But since this was time-based, it took a while to notice.

**If you don't know why something is broken, you're not measuring the right things.**

You don't know what information you'll need to diagnose in the future. But since you might be overwhelmed, let me simplify what to measure.

For every process in your business, keep *logs* (records) of the following:

- The quantities of inputs
- The time the process started
- Cost to run the process
- The time the process ended
- The quantities of outputs

We're measuring quantities, time, and costs for inputs, outputs and running the process (and subprocess).

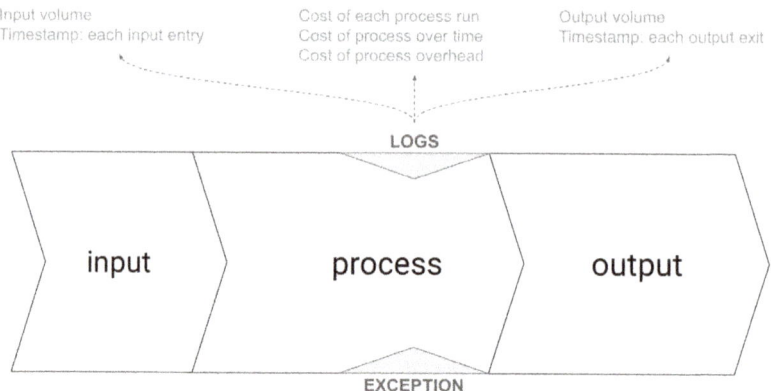

Because you've broken down the business into *input → process → output* you're not confused about what to measure. Every process has the same information to log.

Do you need to measure everything? Sure, it would help, but there's a diminishing return. With digital data, you can collect a lot of information just in case, but for manual processes, too much measurement can slow you down. Here's how to think about it:

- What if you want to measure something that *might* be useful? For example, you're running paid marketing campaigns and you want to track cost per click. That's digital data, easy to collect and store – go ahead and keep it. It might be useful.
- What if the process is drilled down and a quick thing that takes your offshore team 15 minutes, and is not done too often, and the costs of a screw-up are minimal?

Skip measuring unless it's something you're actively diagnosing.

If you're diagnosing problems in the business, you're going to "zoom in" on certain processes as we discussed at the beginning of this chapter. And as you do that, you're also zooming in with your Logs. Which helps you diagnose – because you have numbers.

## Tip: With Problems, Work from Front to Back

I find that a majority of the time, working *front to back* gives me the most success in diagnosing problems. That is, for any given set of processes, unless you have evidence pointing to a specific cause of the problem, start looking for the issue in the *earliest* one in the sequence, then work your way to stages that happen later in time.

The simple reason is that a problem from an earlier step can affect all later steps. So if you start your investigation earlier in the chain, you're more likely to find it.

Remember the issue I had diagnosing declining revenues, and I was tearing my hair out because the sales department stats seemed good? The underlying problem actually happened from a change to an earlier process – our lead generation process.

An important caveat: this chapter is about diagnosing problems. With *problems* it's helpful to work from Front to Back. With *opportunities* covered in the next chapter that isn't always the case.

## When You Still Can't See The Solution

Running the Business Unlock system above will help you diagnose and fix most problems. But what if you still can't see the problem or the solution?

Sometimes you're too close to see it. Maybe it's something outside of your expertise. Time to call in the cavalry.

Often this is where we freeze up. Not only do you have to identify the right person to help you (are they *really* an expert?) but the costs can stack up quickly as a consultant digs in and starts asking questions.

Here's the good news. You already saved a ton of time, money and anxiety by mapping out your business:

- You've clarified the question you're asking, and where in the business things aren't working, which means you can better target the exact expert you need.
- You can vet experts for whether they've solved a problem very similar to the one you have.
- You've broken down your process into segments so the consultant can understand your business quickly.
- You've collected data that will help them zero in on exactly what is wrong.

One of my companies recently had a problem with email deliverability, our messages were going into the spam folder.

Deliverability was so bad that paying customers weren't getting anything from us – and were canceling their orders. We didn't have any email experts on staff, and I don't know anything about email, other than I don't like it. Our email function hadn't been documented to that level of detail, because we use a marketing automation tool.

In other words, we had a problem, but the "zoom level" didn't let us see how to fix it.

I quickly sketched out the inputs and outputs of the process and broke it down into sub-processes with inputs and outputs. We had systems setup, content writing, sending, and replies. I wasn't an email expert, but could see it could be in one of several places:

1. The domain was configured wrong
2. The marketing automation software was configured wrong
3. The content we were putting in some emails was being flagged as spammy, so our transactional emails (receipts, delivery notifications) were also being spamboxed
4. We had been put on a naughty list by some Internet Star Chamber
5. After we sent it, readers were marking us as spam

Now I could have hired a consultant right off the bat, but having broken down the problem I could do a little more homework to get the best, most specific person for a limited problem.

It only took a little checking – chatting with the marketing automation platform support – to see #2 and #4 weren't an issue. But the big black box was #1. Nobody on the team knew anything about it, and that problem could cascade into causing #3 to be a problem (remember the Front to Back tip above).

This made my search for a consultant super targeted: I needed someone who could check our domain configuration, and fix it if necessary. Because I had identified how many emails we were sending (an output to our mailing process), I knew it had to be someone who dealt with domains that sent millions of emails a year, and sent both transactional and marketing messages – so that was added to the screening criteria.

When engaging him, before we even met I could provide what he needed:

- Configuration of the domain (output of the configuration process)
- Email contents (output of the email writing process)
- Email volume (logs of the sending process)
- Unsubscribe rates (logs of the sending process)

The result? It took all of $250 and two half-hour meetings for the right consultant to diagnose and solve the problem. Our emails were out of spam and being read again.

If you're familiar with email problems, you might be thinking

"Yeah that's obvious." But there are things in your business you *aren't* an expert in, and this same methodology can save your bacon. It could be marketing, legal, R&D, accounting, distribution, tax. . . That day will come – and you can think back to this simple example.

## 2.4

# Unlocking Possibilities

So far we've been focused on understanding the business and fixing problems. But the Business Unlock process you're going through also allows you to unlock growth and have a far more valuable business.

Let's start with a reframe of how you can grow, then apply the principles of this book to make it real.

### Seven Levers of Growth

What if I told you that you could use this process to improve your business by 10%? That wouldn't be too exciting, but you'd say "That's doable".

OK, so 10% is doable.

But if I told you we're going to DOUBLE your business, all of a sudden you're thinking "That feels hard." And you'd be right, because you're probably thinking you have to do One Big Thing to double the business.

Let's not get too mathy, but the bottom line: **if you fix just seven smaller things in your business and improve by only 10%, you nearly double the business profits:**

$$1.1 \times 1.1 \times 1.1 \times 1.1 \times 1.1 \times 1.1 \times 1.1 = 1.94x$$

The point is, you don't have to always bite off one big thing and risk choking on it. The times when I've bet everything on one strategy haven't worked out great. That might be your experience too – you have high hopes for a new Big Initiative, spend a bunch of time and money on it, and … it doesn't *really* move the needle. That's normal. But we de-risk growth when we don't go all-in on one thing and instead try several.

Of course, sometimes you'll get more or less improvement than 10%, but let's say you work on only 5 things, two of them get 6% better, one gets 9% better, one gets 10% better, and two get 20% better. You're at 1.94x a different way.

The process mapping you've gone through has given you a firm foundation for your business. A place to stand. Now each one of these 10% improvements increases the leverage you have to grow.

> "Give me a lever and a place to stand and I shall move the world."
> - Archimedes

Where do these 10%s show up in the business mapping you did? Simple: they're increases of 10% in the *outputs* of seven processes in the business. Because we've already modeled the business, we just need to identify the Significant Seven we'll be working on … Then drill into those processes to make them a little better.

## Finding the Biggest Lever

We have our principle: we're going to double the business with 10% improvements to seven processes. Some things won't actually give you leverage – making your web page 10% longer doesn't mean it's 10% better.

When I analyze a company, here are the seven big levers I look at to drive this growth:

1. **Leads:** How many prospects is the company attracting? We define a "lead" as someone who has expressed interest in a solution you have to offer. So someone who is just sorta kinda interested in your stuff and visits your website is not a lead. But someone who has downloaded a PDF that speaks to a specific problem your product solves is a lead.

2. **Conversions:** How many leads are converting into paying customers? If you have salespeople, this is your sales function – taking Leads and selling to them to close deals for revenue. If you're selling online, it would be your purchase flow or cart process. It's how you turn interested people into customers.

3. **Weighted Average Item Price:** What is the *weighted* average price that's being charged? You may have many

products being sold at different price points. Multiply the price point for each product by the quantity sold and that gives you this number. Why are we weighting it? Because if you have one super high-priced item, but only sell one unit a year … and 3 products that are dirt cheap that sell 1,000,000 units – we need to adjust for the volume. It also means fixing this lever could address *either* the prices of the items or the mix of what you're promoting. Note that if you are selling more than one item in a transaction – such as an eCommerce store where multiple items can be ordered at once – you can use AOV (average order value) for this purpose.

4.  **Transactions Per Client:** How many times is a customer paying during their lifetime? Customers who pay more times are worth more (duh). When you're selling individual items, this would be repeat purchases of individual items, improving this lever you're trying to get them to buy more times. If you're selling on monthly subscription billing, it would be the number of months they're on subscription. Improving this lever is about increasing the number of purchases.

5.  **Frequency of Purchase:** How frequently are they purchasing? If it's one-off purchases, can you get them to consume more frequently? Can you put them on a subscription? If you're already offering monthly subscriptions, can you offer a weekly option?

6.  **Margin:** How much profit are we taking? Can we change how we deliver, or what we deliver, to increase

margin? For a products business, this could be changing suppliers or vendors. For service businesses, this could be improving delivery processes or replacing people with technology (shameless shill: I have a business that helps companies do this, for a thank you only for book readers who made it this far visit TheBusinessUnlock. com/resources).

7. **Operating Cash Flow:** how are we generating cash from business operations? I measure this as *cash velocity*. That is, how can we condense the time between when we pay for stuff, and when we get paid by customers? Shrinking this number drastically improves cash flow and allows you to invest in the business. This lever is things like getting payment upfront, pulling in invoice terms from net 60 to net 10, stretching payables from net 30 to net 60, decreasing inventory on hand, etc.

In your business, there may be others – but these are a great starting point that applies to almost every business.

Let's put this into practice for you right now. Below is a worksheet. Rank each of the seven levers in terms of how big an impact it can make, and how easy you think implementing something will be.

- **Impact:** Rank from 1-7, with 7 being "this will have the biggest positive impact on the business" and 1 being "this will have the least impact". For example, you believe increasing the Average Item Price will have the biggest impact, because that will let you upgrade your customer base to less price-sensitive customers, positively impacting transactions per client and frequency of purchase.

- **Ease of Implementation:** Rank from 1-7, with 7 being "this will be easy for us to implement" and 1 being "this will be hard to implement". For example, if your company's skills are in marketing, Leads might be easiest to work on and have the biggest impact. If you don't have internal skills in customer acquisition but are good operationally, perhaps work on Margin.

You're **ranking**, meaning only one Lever can get "1", only one can get "2", etc. in each column. Said another way, in Impact, you cannot repeat any number; the same in Ease of Implementation.

Fill in the first two columns, then multiply them to get a score. No, I did not say there wouldn't be math on the test. Settle down. It's multiplication. If you can't do it, ask a 5th grader.

If you want a downloadable version of this worksheet it's available at TheBusinessUnlock.com/resources

| Lever | Impact (1-7, 7 = biggest positive impact) | Ease of Implementation (1-7, 7 = easiest) | Score (multiply the two) |
|---|---|---|---|
| Leads | | | |
| Conversions | | | |
| Weighted Avg. Item Price | | | |
| Transactions per Client | | | |
| Freq. of Purchase | | | |
| Margin | | | |
| Operating Cash Flow | | | |

Now look at the scores – the higher the number, the more of a priority that lever is. Circle three of them you're going to tackle first. Now, identify all the *processes* in your business map that would need to be examined to implement that change, and list them here:

1. _____

2. _____

3. _____

4. _____

5. _____

## Speed to Money

I tend to find entrepreneurs are either "marketing types" or "sales types" and this can significantly influence where they put their energy into looking for opportunities.

- Marketing types prefer to look at how to get more people interested in the offer, in other words, get people to the sales process.
- Sales types prefer to work on how to get more sales opportunities for customers.

Unfortunately, this tends to bias people towards the thing they *like* rather than the thing that will have the biggest impact.

**You want to work on levers that are closest to the money.** Fortunately, the *logs* you've installed from the Business Unlock will give you the information you need to increase speed to money.

If you are trying to increase revenue rapidly, working on Leads might not be the best thing to do – because those leads take time to filter down to sales. A marketing type would rush off to try shiny new campaigns – when the results of those campaigns will take longer to turn into money.

Sales types default to tweaking their sales scripts, looking for a better conversion rate. But that isn't always ideal – for instance, a lot of smaller businesses selling higher-ticket offers do 2-3 sales pitches per month – and even if they improve it by 50% (let alone

10%) they won't notice if it made a difference because the dataset is so small. So for growth possibilities, sometimes it's best to look "front to back" and sometimes "back to front".

The short of it is, you need to be able to reliably measure the results of what you are improving, or else you're flying blind. Good thing you have logs.

Here's the general way of thinking about this:

- If you have fewer than 10 sales pitches per month, focus on marketing to get more sales "at bats" first.
- If you have more than 30 sales pitches per month, focus on sales first to get more revenue now.
- If it's between those two, pick what you like. Or, better yet, do both – just make sure you're measuring them independently.

## Mo' Money

I kind of tricked you in the first part of this chapter. I sold you by telling you that you'll double your business. I lied. You'll actually do far better.

By going through the Business Unlock process, you've just increased the value of your *business asset* by a lot more than double. That's because when a business is sold, it's usually valued on a formula, which is simplified as:

$$V = P \times M$$

(Yes, more multiplication. Buy a stack of candy bars to bribe that 5th grader)

That is, the *Value* of your business is worth the *Profits* times a *Multiple*. What are these things?

- **Profits:** This is how much money the company makes after all expenses. If we're being fancy, this is EBITDA (earnings before interest, taxes, depreciation and amortization), but for shorthand and especially for smaller businesses, you can think of it as profit after you pay all your bills.
- **Multiple:** This is a number based on "how likely does the buyer think they can turn the price they pay for the business into more money". It's affected by industry, company size, and – very importantly – *risk*. So smaller companies have lower multiples because generally speaking, they're more risky. Likewise, if the owner is essential to the business it will get a lower multiple. In very small businesses the multiple could be 0.8x or less (if the business makes $100k in EBITDA, it might be 0.8 and the valuation $80,000). In a mid-size enterprise, it could be 3-5x.

A full discussion on this would take more pages than you care to read, but here's the headline: **increasing your multiple has**

**a bigger impact on the value of your business than profit …
and the Business Unlock process increases <u>both</u> profit and
multiple.**

We looked at profit increase with the seven levers above, but what
about increasing the multiple? The entire process we're going
through in this book de-risks a company:

1. The business becomes fully documented so a buyer knows
   it's a machine that works.
2. One of the biggest negative impacts on multiples is
   "owner is essential in the business" … but now you have
   processes around what you are doing – so you can replace
   yourself and increase your multiple.
3. No single employee can cause the company to implode by
   leaving (called "key man risk"), which increases certainty
   for the buyer.
4. You have visibility into the business with Logs. Buyers
   will know they can fix problems easily.
5. You have documented exceptions so a buyer's fear of
   unknowns is decreased.
6. With the seven levers, you've increased profits.

Let's pretend you would have gotten a multiple of 3x when you
started reading this book. It could be more, could be less, but
let's just assume that. Even if you *never* increased revenue, the
Business Unlock process could easily take you to a 5x multiple.
That means if your company was generating $500,000 in profit

(and that didn't change) – the value of your business went from $1,500,000 to $2,500,000.

But of course, you're also working on the seven levers. Let's pretend you had hiccups along the way and only increased profit 1.5x, not the full 1.94x. Your $500,000 profit business is now generating $750,000 in profit. And even better, it's now worth $3,750,000.

You just created $2.25M in enterprise value, and $250k in yearly profit, by just following a defined process. And this works at every scale and size of business – just adjust the starting multiple. Not bad.

## 2.5

# The One-Hour Unlock

"I'm sick of reading, Raj. How do I make this real NOW?"

I'm so glad you asked. If you aren't predisposed to taking action, I'm going to challenge you: it's time to go from consumption to creation right now. In this chapter, we're going to do a jump start of the Business Unlock process to get you results as fast as possible.

Right now, at least one of the following things is true:

a) *Time* is the problem: you don't have time to do anything, so you're deadlocked from making progress,
b) *Mental Space* is the problem: you're frazzled, running in too many directions, maybe hate your company, or
c) *Clarity* is the problem: you have the time and mental space but don't know how to begin installing this in your business.

Jump to the section below that's relevant to your situation and let's get cranking.

## Time is my Problem

There are many versions of this exercise, mine is simplified. If you're deadlocked for time it's because of one of the reasons on this list:

1. You're doing shit that doesn't need to be done by you

Yes, there's only one thing on that list.

The bottom line is, if you're routinely spending 80+ hours a week grinding on your business, you need to either delegate things or stop doing things. Have I worked long hours? Absolutely, in sprints.

*If your norm is working insane hours so you can't find the time to improve your situation, you must delegate, defer, and dump tasks until you can.*

Take this as an axiom: if you don't have 10 hours a week to work on making your business better, something is wrong, and some things have to go. Start by asking yourself these four questions (a downloadable version of this is available at TheBusinessUnlock. com/resources):

1. What am I doing now that won't really move the needle *now?* Examples: daily social media posting, blogging, and redesigning a website. Anything that doesn't directly

generate revenue *now* or isn't a contractual commitment is game.

_____

_____

_____

_____

_____

_____

2. What delivery work am I doing for customers/clients? If I was sick for a month, who could I get who would do this work?

_____

_____

_____

_____

_____

_____

3. What are all the things I'm doing now that are taking more than 5 hours a week? Who could I delegate it to (whether or not I have that person available now, or even can afford them now)?

_____

_____

_____

_____

_____

_____

4.  What are all the things I'm doing that are worth less than
    $10 per hour? Who could I delegate it to (whether or not
    I have that person available now, or even can afford them
    now)?

_____

_____

_____

_____

_____

_____

By now you should have some ideas for the areas that are blocking
you, even if you don't yet have a solution for them. Now let's free
up some time. We're going to go through everything above and
designate it with one of three statuses:

*   **Dump:** go through the above list and cross out anything
    that doesn't need to be done now, based on the state of
    your business today. If it won't matter in the next six
    months, dump it. If it's important again later, you can
    consider it. But get rid of it now.

- **Defer:** go through the list and cross out things that might make a difference, but you can pause for a month or two and the business won't grind to a halt.
- **Delegate:** circle everything on the list which (1) you can delegate to someone you're already paying for today (team member, contractor, etc), (2) can be done by someone being paid less than $10/hour (such as a virtual assistant).

The Dump and Defer items, we're not going to worry about right now. They're not important.

For the Delegate items, give everything away you can. Use people on your team. Once you've exhausted that bench, get a virtual assistant and delegate things to them.

I don't advocate waiting to get an assistant. My bottom line is this: if you are going to run a business, you need an assistant. Period. They might only be 10 hours a week, but you need one.

*The job of the assistant is to free not only your calendar, but free your* mind *from thinking about the hundreds of little tasks that are collectively eating your time and clogging your creativity.*

## Mental Space is my Problem

There are parts of your business you hate. Admit it. We all have them. And like things that steal your time, the things you hate steal your energy and mental space. When you're irritated by them, it's hard to make progress because you're always being sucked into a bad mental place.

There are two kinds of things that drain your mental energy: *activities* and *people*. In this exercise, take a few minutes to write down what those energy drains are in the first column. Then, for each one write down what the ideal outcome would be to free yourself from it and one thing you can calendar right now to begin that process.

You get to paint your own picture here. If Gordo With the Man Bun in Marketing irritates you every day and you dream of cutting that hair nodule off his head just for spite, it's fine that the ideal outcome is to replace him.

| Energy Drain (activities or people) | Ideal Outcome | First Action & When |
|---|---|---|
|  |  |  |
|  |  |  |
|  |  |  |
|  |  |  |
|  |  |  |
|  |  |  |
|  |  |  |

*Need more space? Download a worksheet at TheBusinessUnlock.com/resources*

Now that you've filled in the chart, you aren't done. Open up your calendar and transfer the first action onto the calendar so it's not trapped here. Then tell your assistant to bug you every week until it's done.

## Clarity is my Problem

If you have the time and mental space for the Business Unlock, congratulations. It's time to get this put in place fast.

But I have bad news.

That is: you're not a superhero. I'm sorry, I know your mom said you're amazing – but you can't do everything at once at super speed. *What this means is if you try to implement this all yourself, you will fail.*

Many business operators decide this project is something where they need to be involved from beginning to end, drawing up all the processes. Done this way, not only will you have someone in charge (you?) who isn't the most familiar with each process, but it robs the organization of being invested in the process.

The right way to implement it is to have the **person doing the thing document the thing**. Now that might be you, for some things (but fewer, since you have delegated some in the Time section above, right?). But if you're not the one doing it, you should not be the one documenting it.

So how is this the One Hour Unlock?

Because I'm going to give you materials so you can delegate the creation of the entire system to your team in an hour. This will not only free you from Yet Another Big Project That Probably Won't Get Done, but will make your company more valuable because the processes become a part of its fabric – not imposed from above and resisted.

Years ago, I screwed this up. I knew I needed processes developed – so I told everyone they had to document everything they were doing. The reaction was swift and nasty: "You're having us document our jobs so you can fire us!" Today, it might echo as "You're having us document our jobs so AI can replace us!"

Honestly, that could be true now or down the road. But that uncomfortable truth can't stop you from doing the single most important exercise you've ever done to increase both the value of your business and your ease running it.

Instead, we need them to understand that life will be *better for them and their colleagues* when they do it. The good thing is, that's also true. Once the team has documented everything this way they will have more clarity and potential for growth in their roles.

Here's one way I've found successful for socializing this project. You can swipe this message and send it to your team, or (far better) socialize it in an all-hands meeting face to face.

(If you want a copy-and-paste version, it's downloadable at TheBusinessUnlock.com/resources)

It's really important that everyone here be able to take vacations unplugged, or if a loved one gets sick we can take time off without feeling conflicted about having to be 'on call' because we're the only one who can handle something. We're launching a project to make sure that if you ever need coverage, you can take your personal time without stress to you or your co-workers. When we've completed this project we'll also have a lot more clarity of what's expected of everyone on the team, and as your leadership team, we can make sure you're rewarded for going above and beyond.

For each task you have in your job, we'd like you to fill in a short questionnaire that will kick off this project. You'll need to make copies of this questionnaire for each task you do in your job.

### QUESTIONNAIRE

Write all of these from the perspective of "If you're on vacation, and someone was covering this task for you, what would they need to know to not disturb you on vacation?" Assume they've never done the job before, so they have no context at all.

1.  What does someone else need to give to you to do this task? List everything the person covering for you should expect. Information, documents, passwords, parts, etc.

2.  What are all of the pieces of information needed to do this task? Where is this information kept? Please be specific, like including links.

3.  If someone covering for you needed to look up information about what you did so they don't bother you on vacation, where would they do that? Where do you record all your tasks and their status?

4.  What information should the person covering for you write down, and where should they store it, so when you come back you are organized and don't have to figure out what they did?

5.  What are situations where sometimes you can't proceed further on this task but need to call someone? Who do you need to call?

6.  When you're done with this task, what happens to the work product? Where do you put it, or who do you send it to? What format does it need to be in?

    Your teammates are also doing this exercise so everyone can help each other. Whenever you interface with other team members in your job, meet to ensure the information you're getting from them or giving them lines up in your questionnaires.

Let's take a closer look at the questionnaire, and why each question is there. Each one gets to a core element of the Business Unlock process:

1. What does someone else need to give to you to do this task? List everything the person covering for you should expect. Information, documents, passwords, parts, etc.

2. What are all of the pieces of information needed to do this task? Where is this information kept? Please be specific, like including links.

Questions 1 and 2 collect the *inputs* necessary for a process. In other words, anything that someone doing the process needs.

3. If someone covering for you needed to look up information about what you did so they don't bother you on vacation, where would they do that? Where do you record all your tasks and their status?

4. What information should the person covering for you write down, and where should they store it, so when you come back you are organized and don't have to figure out what they did?

Questions 3 and 4 document the *logs* of a process. What information needs to be kept so the process is efficient.

5. What are situations where sometimes you can't proceed further on this task but need to call someone? Who do you need to call?

Question 5 documents *exceptions* for a process. What happens when things go wrong.

6.  When you're done with this task, what happens to the work product? Where do you put it, or who do you send it to? What format does it need to be in?

Question 6 documents *output* of a process.

With these six questions and a few instructions, you've had people document all the processes of your business.

If you have multiple levels of management, start with the top level of managers and work your way down the hierarchy. Whenever a manager's job involves delegating something, that's a sub-process.

For example, if AJ runs marketing and has three direct reports (a team member for paid media, one for content, and one for analytics), she would document the things she does, and the responsibilities of her team are subprocesses. AJ then documents what she does interfacing with other departments and coordinating things, and for each of her three direct reports, she'd have a subprocess that's a blank.

AJ then delegates the documentation to her three direct reports, ensuring their documentation (*inputs* and *outputs*) lines up with their teammates and with her own. AJ's responsibility is to make sure all those connections make sense, and that each team member has used an appropriate level of "zoom" in their processes so that if they were sick, AJ or one of her team members could step in and substitute for the ill team member.

Next, you need to make this documentation useful – storing it in a playbook. There should be one, single repository for all the processes. It doesn't matter what system you use (electronic, paper, stone tablets) so long as it meets these requirements:

- It's centralized so management can see everything
- Individual team members can update their processes as things change
- If there are confidentiality concerns, you can limit certain parts of it to appropriate levels in the organization

If you want a free online template for your playbook, you can download one at TheBusinessUnlock.com/resources

What we've done here is take the load off your shoulders as much as possible. You may not be a superhero who can get all of this done, but you'll feel like one.

# Make Growth Inevitable:
# The Unlock Flywheel

The biggest lump of work is installing the system in your business the first time. Once you've done that – even if you've done a poor job – things get much, much easier. In this chapter, we'll look at how you can spend just a little time maintaining the system and see growth.

## Management by Vacation

For over a decade I've coached founders using a concept I call "Management by Vacation." The premise is simple: as an owner, you should be *separate* from your business. In other words, you should be able to go on vacation and the business should keep growing without you. Not only does this give you ultimate freedom, but your company will maximize its valuation (See "Mo' Money" in Chapter 4 above).

There's one other benefit that founders often overlook. Your team might be happier if you're not always around. Founders tend to tinker, come up with new ideas, and generally make things *less* stable once a company reaches a certain level of maturity. Because the "machine" of the company has been documented, the team won't feel they need you swooping in to save the day all the time. If you're showing up to work and nobody needs you – it's a good thing.

Here's the protocol:

Plan a one-week, fully unplugged vacation. Zero contact is permitted with the office. Think about what will break if you do that, and make sure your processes cover them. Take the vacation, and see what breaks, and what things were "held" for you to handle when you return.

Create *input → process → output* systems for each of those things, without you in the process.

This is important, control freaks. You're going to let things break. You have to. Unless the team understands nobody is coming to save them, they'll resort to having you swoop in to save the day.

Then do the same thing for a two-week fully unplugged vacation.

Then one month.

Then one quarter.

Then one year.

Yes, it's possible – because each time you're documenting and replacing your brain with systems. Systems that can include the brains of other people, processes, and technology.

The more mature your business is, the easier it is to extend your absence. I own one business where I can check in yearly. One where I could be unplugged for a month. And a startup where I could unplug for two weeks, but it wouldn't grow if I did. For each organization, I look to extend the time I can be absent, empower the team, and get out of the way.

## The Flywheel For Startups

Startups – that is, companies that haven't defined their growth machine, often can't have founders checking out for long periods of time. The reason is, there is simply too much being made up as the company is being built. In other words, processes are changing rapidly.

However, that doesn't mean you should avoid documenting business processes.

Wait, why should I go through this whole process if it's just going to change? Shouldn't I nail it down first, before wasting energy on this? That's what I used to think, too.

In the startup context, documenting serves a different purpose:

1. By documenting a process *before* you implement it, you're taking the time to think through how you want it to work. Remember in science class when they made you write down your hypothesis, and then test it? Well, that's a startup. A set of hypotheses, and a set of tests. If you don't document what you're testing – you won't capture learnings as crisply.

2. When things break – and in startups, they break all the time – you need to be able to quickly diagnose what broke and why. If you've been good about documenting *inputs* → *process* → *output*, *logs* and *exceptions* described in this book, you'll be able to spot these problems easily.

> **Note:** I've written extensively about how to use the scientific method to scale a business, you can find free resources on my personal site: rajjha.com

Here's how startups should use the Business Unlock system for growth:

Use the framework in this book to document the business at a very high level. Pay particular attention to anything you're outsourcing: for example, if you've got an agency running your paid media – ensure you've got good logs of performance so you know if problems are with their services, or your product/offer.

Don't try to exhaustively document the entire company. Instead, zoom in on:

1. Anything that *won't* change – processes you want to "set and forget". By locking those down, you can focus your attention on validating the hypothesis of the business model without worrying that routine things are getting done.

2. The one thing you're testing right now. Whatever you're working on – whether it be your sales process, the offer to the market, product, or manufacturing – zoom in on that area and start refining how you're doing it now. This will help you diagnose what's not working, and see opportunities to make it better. Instead of making decisions about what to try as you zig-zag to success, you (and the whole team) will be on the same page.

## The Flywheel for Mature Businesses

Mature businesses have the opportunity to not only "run on rails" using the Business Unlock process, but to grow while giving the owner more freedom. Here is the process you can install in the business to maximize both after you've done your initial documentation:

1. **Monthly Process Audit:** Every month, each team member should check to see if any processes have been created or changed. If they have, schedule a time to document them (or update the documentation). This ensures that the company playbook is up to date.

2. **Quarterly One Biggest Problem:** Every function in a

business has One Biggest Problem at a given time. Every quarter, leadership should identify what that problem is (for example, lead generation is underperforming by 17%). Then, use the Business Unlock principles to solve it by asking these questions:

   a. Is the cause clear from the processes as documented? If not, re-work the documentation by "zooming in."

   b. Do we have enough data in our Logs to diagnose it? If not, add more Logs.

   c. Can changes to process solve the problem? This could be changing how things are done, who is doing them, or even taking chunks of the business and outsourcing them.

3. **Annual Zero-Base Teardown:** Every year, add a process to challenge the processes in place. Have each manager review all the processes in their scope and answer the following questions:

   a. Which processes are no longer contributing to the goals of my department?

   b. Which processes are inefficient and could be improved? How?

   c. Which processes have poor documentation that needs to be shored up?

   d. Which processes can be replaced with technology?

   e. If I had to rebuild the processes in my department from scratch, would I do it the same way? If not, how would I change them?

# PART THREE

# AI & AUTOMATION

My friend Josh's business is dead. He just doesn't know it yet. He runs an agency that creates marketing materials for businesses. Most of his agency's work is generating blog posts, newsletters, and other content. The work they do is really great.

For over a year I've been telling him that his business is going to need a complete rehaul, fast, if it's going to survive. That's because other than the relationship aspect, and (at least for a little while) the strategy piece, the cost of generating content is going to zero.

In other words, someone will be able to offer software or a service that costs a fraction of what Josh's agency charges. His headcount is a liability.

This means Josh needs to hit a hard reset and disrupt himself using AI tools before someone else does it.

It's an extreme case, but I can point to examples in any industry. Let's look at how you can unlock leverage in your business with automation & AI.

# Getting Started With AI & Automation

If you get serious about automation, it's a huge lever – I've worked with businesses that have cut costs by over 26%, or been able to create entirely new business functions, without hiring anybody.

Best of all, the CEO sleeps better at night since the automations *just run* without hiring and HR headaches.

After implementing the process in Part Two of this book, you probably see a lot you can automate. You can take a look at each process, "zoom in" to the right level, and find technology that can do things that people are doing now.

For example, you might have a process where an unlucky human is tasked with copying files from one software platform into another – something perfect for automation. Or, you might have a person making judgment calls ("Is this customer prospect qualified?") that could be handled easily by an AI.

Before You Do, Delete

But let's take a beat before you run off and automate things. There's one step to make this easier.

**That's finding what you can *delete*.**

A few years ago I was helping a business I invested in to map its processes. I was pleased to see the founder was keeping a lot of data – good logs. He was being smart about the Business Unlock. Or was he?

Two years before, he wanted more visibility into sales and asked for reports weekly – then stopped looking at them when the sales process changed. Many months and wasted man-hours later, the team was dutifully generating reports – that nobody was looking at.

We call this "cruft" – things that got added over time but serve no useful purpose anymore. Before automating I want you to think through one important filter: "What should I STOP doing?" There's no point in automating something you shouldn't be doing at all. Logging stuff that doesn't matter is also a waste of resources.

Once you start deleting things that don't need to be done or taking a hard look at how they are being done, I'll bet you find a lot you'd change. The great thing is, even if you never automate – you already chalked up a win and your team will be thanking you for eliminating pointless work.

## IT'S AUTOMATION TIME: THE PROCESS

The way to think about automation is doing it in waves. Don't try to automate everything at once, because the project is too big and you'll give up without making progress. Instead, we're going to start with the thing that will give you the biggest impact. Once that's done, we'll repeat the process – find the thing with the biggest impact, and solve it. By iterating this way you're advancing down the list from biggest to smallest – and if conditions change and a new Biggest Thing comes up, that gets slotted at the top. That way you're seeing big results as fast as possible.

Here's the process:

### 1.  Identify Best Candidates for Automation

For each process you created in Part Two – make a list of the ones that are *frequent, routine,* and *have high cost.* That's the list to tackle first. For example, if you're generating a lot of content in your business and have high-priced writers – can you replace some or all of that with AI writing?

In one of my businesses, we were generating dozens of images per week for testing Facebook ads – which was very manual and took expensive agency time. This was a perfect candidate for automation – frequent (weekly), routine (doing the same thing sometimes 100 times a week), and high cost (manual labor creating images).

## 2. Define Automation Inputs and Outputs

If you've already implemented the systems I suggested in Part Two, this might already be done: documenting the *inputs* and *outputs* of a process. But if you haven't done that yet, now is when you'll define what you want the automation to produce, and the information/materials it needs to be given to produce it. It's fine if you don't know whether something exists to do this – I'll show you why in a second.

The point here is to say "Instead of a person doing this task, I'm automating this process. I give the process this information: _____; and the result of the automation is this: _____"

For my process with the images, my desired input and output was "every week we input creative direction and the output is 100 images meeting the creative direction requirements, sized at 1080x1080 in JPG format" – and in that case, AI image generation with a light layer of human oversight was perfect, replacing a lot of manual graphic design.

## 3. Find Automation Solutions

Last, you're going to research how those things could be automated. Or, better yet, find a colleague who might have already done the research. You'd be amazed at how much can be automated – but it's often not easy to find, so having someone who's an expert or in your same industry who's done it can make a huge difference.

If you don't have any buddies who are automation/AI experts, there are a ton of consultants who can help – and a good one will be well worth the investment in terms of cost savings. There are also resources at TheBusinessUnlock.com/resources to help you in the search.

### MANAGING AUTOMATIONS: BEWARE

When you're automating business processes, it's important to have a system that can manage them for you. Otherwise, you can get a tangled mess of systems, each doing pieces of the puzzle. I see this with companies where there are semi-technical people implementing automations, and all of a sudden there are dozens of Zapier sequences gluing things together and nobody remembers how to fix them if anything breaks or changes.

Because there are so many systems one could use to manage automations, instead of telling you which one to use, I'll give you a list of things your system needs to do. This way you'll know if your current software will work, or know how to choose a system if you don't have one.

Not surprisingly, these principles map to the Business Unlock process in Part Two because they're fundamental to good process design and implementation.

1. **Unlimited Nesting:** This is principle #2 of this book. The software should be able to break down big processes into

smaller processes. That's because when you're automating, you'll often be automating smaller parts to start – then automating more as technology gets better. Importantly, the nesting shouldn't have a limit ("only three levels of sub-processes are allowed"), because that could make you hit a wall when you're automating and need more levels.

2.  **Robots On The Team:** The software should treat each task as something that can be done by people, AI, or other systems it's connected to. If you're using a system that's really made for people – and automation and AI is an afterthought – the software won't let you automate to the extent you want. Unfortunately, most workflow management, task management and project management systems fail at this.

3.  **Non-Techy Friendly:** automations should be "one-click simple". You want your team to be able to use it quickly and easily. Almost as if the automation is another team member. If you need to hire a developer to automate and then train people, not only is it expensive, but it means there's more friction when you want to update or improve a process.

If you want to learn what systems I've found that fit these criteria, visit TheBusinessUnlock.com/resources.

(p.s.: shameless plug: my software, atomized.ai, fits all these criteria).

# Protecting Yourself From HAL-9000

In *2001: A Space Odyssey,* the HAL-9000, an AI system tasked with running a spaceship decides the humans on board are in the way of his mission, so he tries to kill them. He disconnects life support, pulls one astronaut's air supply – and attempts to lock Dave Bowman, the last remaining crew member, out of the ship.

Of course, that's a science fiction AI. But fiction can help us think about problems that might arise in the real world, right now.

In Part Two of this book we were introduced to Rogue Robot. He's an incredibly helpful robot, but he's also a rascal – if you aren't *painfully* explicit in giving him what he needs, he'll just make stuff up.

We didn't go into detail about why this is the case, but it's because Rogue Robot is a *probabilistic* AI. He might be well-intentioned, but ultimately he's making guesses about what you want. Inside his silicon brain, he's guessing "Is this more likely to be the right answer than that?" to arrive at what is *likely* the right decision … But it might not be.

We humans tend to think of our businesses *deterministically* (if-this-then-that). We come from a mechanistic world, where when we turn the doorknob, we expect the door to open. We don't expect the doorknob to consider whether we want it to open, and if it thinks "Yeah, that's what he wants" let us in. Unfortunately, we're now using a tool that makes guesses, not follows rules.

In *2001* we see this same tension: as HAL-9000 starts to act slightly erratically, the humans discuss shutting him down. We humans expect robots to be rule-based (deterministic) machines.

**This is fundamental to the Business Unlock process, and your success as an entrepreneur.** We want our processes to be reliable. A given input, when given to a process, yields a predictable output. If you don't adhere to this principle, your business will forever be a mystery.

For example, you might have told Rogue Robot to answer your customer support emails, and given him examples of how to answer. As in, "If a customer asks about how to get a refund, tell them to mail the product back to this address along with a copy of their receipt." When Rogue Robot gets an email and determines the customer is asking about a refund, he'll send the appropriate message.

But the thing is, sometimes he'll be wrong.

He might get a qualitative judgment request from a customer. "Is your return policy better than Amazon's?" – Rogue Robot doesn't have enough information about this, but he knows the customer is talking about return policies. He guesses that the customer is looking for a response about getting refunds – and replies with instructions on how to send a product back. Which isn't what the customer asked. Pissed customer.

This highlights the problem we have with probabilistic AIs. If you could predict every situation, with its nuances, then you might be able to make up rules to keep the robot helpful. But you can't. There are so many edge cases that we can't anticipate when we're dealing with a robot that makes guesses. The same thing that makes probabilistic AIs so useful (it's a compact way of getting the right answer, usually) is the thing that creates the problem.

Let's extend this thinking down the slippery slope.

You've given your customer support function to Rogue Robot, and done your very best to anticipate every situation possible. You've fed in three years of support tickets handled by humans so Rogue Robot has examples of all kinds of situations, everything from product questions, to returns, to refunds.

And, just like you might tell a human support agent, you tell Rogue Robot that it's very important to treat the customer kindly, so they always have a good impression of the company when delivering support. Maybe you use the same principle as I do in my ecommerce business – 'treat them like they're your grandmother.'

So what does Rogue Robot do? He decides that grandma is the most important person in the world – and the best way to make every customer happy is to issue a refund to every customer who ever bought, and let them keep the product. Delighted grannies, across the land!

The infuriating robot thinks he's done what you wanted, and your company has just gone out of business.

Now of course this is an extreme scenario, but it's not beyond the realm of possibility. The more we let AIs make decisions with probabilistic algorithms, the more we can run into these problems.

Remember, the entire point of the Business Unlock – and your whole goal as an owner, is to *increase* certainty. And we've just risked the opposite.

## The Problem of Compounding Mistakes

There's one more thing to think about with AIs: as we have them do things repeatedly, even if they're relatively accurate it still can result in big problems. Let's say that we've done a great job of training our support AI, so it's 99.99% accurate. In other words, it only makes a mistake 0.01% of the time. Pretty good, right?

Now we unleash it on our support channel where it's answering 100 support tickets per day and sit back delighted that we have a 24x7 team member answering tickets in just seconds.

But: what are the odds that it's going to make a mistake in the next 12 months? Unfortunately, that number is pretty high. It's over 98% that it WILL make a mistake. We're virtually assured that using the AI will result in an error. And unfortunately, we don't know how big the error will be. However, since it's likely an edge case, it might be a doozy.

That's why we need to be careful about how we deploy AIs and the magnitude of the problems that could occur. Then, we should think about putting *bumpers* on it so we don't end up with a company-killing event.

I call it "putting a deterministic wrapper on a probabilistic tool," and one of my companies (atomized.ai) was created to address just this mismatch between how people think about their company's functions and how AIs try to guess what we intend.

The takeaway from this: using probabilistic AI is incredibly helpful. But if you're going to do it, and want a predictable business, a process that deploys it should have a deterministic check-and-balance. Said another way: if a robot is guessing, make sure there's checking.

# This Isn't Like Last Time

*"Restaurants don't need to take credit cards"*
*"Businesses don't need a website"*
*"You don't need to use AI in your business"*

Does the third one feel different?

In 1999, I confused my parents – why leave a perfectly good job at a law firm for ... a startup internet company?

When we went public they were happy but (I imagine) pretty skeptical. The Internet was just a passing phase, and their son had bought into a fad. The dot com crash of 2000 proved them right, because we all know the Internet went away.

Oh, wait.

Some things are obvious in retrospect. Credit cards were once a passing fad. Until they weren't and now using cash is weird.

The Internet was uncomfortable in 1999, and having a website was a 'nice to have'. Businesses didn't like the idea that they had to hire a Web Guy. But the companies who leaned in were first to a land grab that gave them an edge for a decade.

New businesses started, Internet-first, and billions of dollars went from incumbents to startups and the few who leaned into adoption.

You're hearing the buzz about AI, and reading conflicting reports about whether this is the Next Big Thing or just a passing fad. History is about to repeat itself.

In *Technological Revolutions and Financial Capital: The Dynamics of Bubbles and Golden Ages*, Professor Carlota Perez gives a framework for why we see financial boom and bust cycles in technology. The interesting part to me isn't the bubble (fools rush in) and bust (pronouncing a fad technology dead). It's the lateral thought: that **a financial bubble driven by speculators *doesn't* invalidate the usefulness of a tool**. Often it's a *timing* mismatch of investment interest and commercial viability. The Internet did change everything for companies that used the tool, even if many of the financial investments in 1999 went to zero.

AI has had several gold rushes already – the difference is that today, right now, companies are already using AI to drastically reduce costs and increase their capabilities. There are actual use cases you can see, regardless of where the financial hype cycle is. Better yet, as we've seen in earlier chapters this tool slots into the universal principles of the Business Unlock.

My kids call me old – but one of the advantages of seeing multiple technology booms and busts is pattern recognition. As I'll illustrate below, we are now past the point of "let's wait and see." Using AI in business is the biggest opportunity we've seen in decades.

If you're like the hundreds of entrepreneurs I've interviewed about how they're experimenting with AI in their business, you've done the same thing. You tried using ChatGPT to replace menial writing, and perhaps try using built-in AI features in the software you're already using. You've made a great start. But that isn't a *process*.

If you're in the top 50% of these businesses, you've built processes where your team uses AI tools to accelerate their work. You *think* you're getting massive leverage because you've started using AI tools that are being rolled out in your current tech stack. Your marketing platform, your CMS, whatever. AI is a part of your process.

But you forget: EVERYONE ELSE HAS THOSE TOO.

Just "using AI" is not a differentiator. When you use a tool that everyone else can, that's not getting ahead. That's table stakes, because a competitor could quite easily do the same thing. Just like any competitor can use a spreadsheet (which was newfangled in the 90s), now they can have their team use ChatGPT to write marketing copy, install an AI chatbot for support, or whatever easy thing you've already done.

Using AI in a way that will truly get you ahead means it needs to be:

- Uniquely tailored to *your* business operations, not a generic tool
- Trained on *your* datasets, not using the default data that anyone can use
- An asset *you* own, not you just renting a feature from a SaaS platform

The breakout winners aren't going to be the companies taking the easy way and upgrading $29 for the "AI Pro" version of off-the-shelf software. They're the ones thinking about what it means to create a process no competitor could have. They're challenging assumptions about how they've operated the business in the past.

Which folds perfectly into everything you learned in Part Two of this book. By following the system I've laid out there, you've already done the heavy lifting that most companies never do. You're perfectly positioned to make the maximal use of AI, and as new technologies are developed you can be the first to drop them into your organization.

Here's why:

1. You defined what's unique about how your company operates in terms of *inputs*, *processes* and *outputs*. Instead of focusing on company operations based on headcount,

you focused on business functions. You can look at any function and ask "Is this best done by a machine or a person?"

2. You are collecting relevant data from the organization in *logs* which lets you diagnose problems and spot opportunities. This means you can train AI tools on data specific to your business. Unlike others who rely on generic tools, your AIs can get smarter with specific context. This means not only improved performance, but you've generated a technology asset that increases your company's valuation (see the discussion "Mo' Money" in Part Two, Chapter 4).

3. You've documented exceptions, so you know where to put 'bumpers' on AIs because they might go off the rails. Think of these as your early warning systems that something might be amiss. This is part of the 'deterministic wrapper' discussed in the previous chapter.

So congratulations – by following the process in this book, you've not only made your company better, but you've future-proofed it.

So now that you've systematized the business properly – how do you choose which AI (or other) technologies to adopt, and when?

## 3.4

# It's About The Adoption, Not The Technology

My cousin Sean runs a lawn care business. We've never talked about it, but I bet he doesn't care much about technology. And that's a good thing because the latest in AI won't make much of a difference to Sean's Lawns. He has the luxury of not caring.

However, your situation is not the same as Sean's. I'm not referring to the fact that it's likely you don't have epic heavy metal hair like he does. I mean he's in an industry and has competition which won't force change. You're probably not.

So how should we decide when it's time to care? If you pay attention to what the press is saying, AI adoption is either:

- "the next big thing" that will dominate the world in the next two years, or …
- nothing to see here, it's just a sideshow parlor trick and maybe it will be vaguely useful in 10 years.

In this case, I ask: what if both were true?

That's the real story of technology adoption. Some people, companies, and industries will push the boundaries and get a competitive advantage. Some won't, and their company will join Blockbuster Video in the tar pits. And some, like Sean's Lawns, won't … and it won't matter.

> "The future is already here – it's just not evenly distributed."
> – William Gibson

So the questions to ask are: in *your* situation, with *your* industry and *your* competitors:

- Threat: What's the bare minimum to stay competitive?
- Opportunity: What would I need to do to outperform my competition?

We don't have to understand everything about the technology. This is a good thing, because AI is moving so fast and is so complicated that it's not possible to understand everything. I'm in the AI industry with a software product and can't keep up.

**Instead, we can focus on *people*** – because the limiting factor for every business will be how we, as meat popsicles, adopt the technology – not the technology itself. Sean can look at his competitors, realize none of them will be adopting any AI stuff for the foreseeable future, and continue rocking on. In my eCommerce business, I need to be thinking about technology with a 1-2 year outlook. In my software business, every week.

This simplifies things considerably because it becomes a behavioral question (how do people act in the face of new technology), not a technological one (predicting what it will be). We can look at how other technologies were adopted.

# 3.5

# How People Adopt Technology

Let's start with how people adopt technology since companies are made of people (for now. We'll talk about the Zero Person Company later). How people behave rolls up into how companies adopt technology.

You youngsters don't remember life before email – but I remember how reluctant people were to use it, afraid that it wasn't secure. For years people preferred the good-old and safe fax machine. Besides, they worked, so why change? (They still won't die – last week my insurance company asked me to fax them something. In 2024. WTF.)

The same thing happened as electricity was introduced into homes. Some people believed the electromagnetic fields generated by the wiring would lead to widespread illness. Besides, candles worked, so why change? … Until enough early adopters installed power and people got used to the idea.

What does this tell us about human nature?

- We don't trust new things easily
- "It works, why change?"
- Once we see enough other monkeys doing it, it becomes "dude, let's fucking go"

The last point is the most interesting one. Email still isn't secure. Nothing's really changed there, but we got over it and started using the tool. We just needed to see enough other simians doing it to not worry. Monkey see, monkey do.

# 3.6

# How Companies Adopt Technology

Remember we're examining how companies adopt technology through the lens of the people who comprise it.

In the book *Diffusions of Innovation*, Everett Roger gives a much-cited model for technology adoption. He breaks down organizations into different categories based on when they adopt technology. Innovators adopt it first but are a small percentage of the overall industry. Early adopters go next as a larger percentage of the industry, all the way down to the Laggards who adopt late.

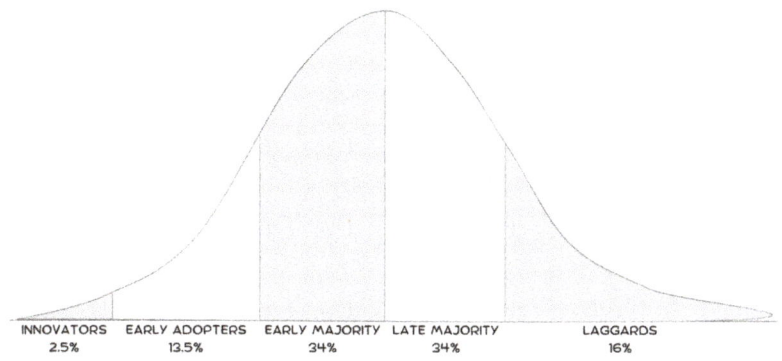

| INNOVATORS | EARLY ADOPTERS | EARLY MAJORITY | LATE MAJORITY | LAGGARDS |
|---|---|---|---|---|
| 2.5% | 13.5% | 34% | 34% | 16% |

We're trying to answer the questions "What's the bare minimum to stay competitive?" and "What would I need to do to outperform my competition?" and eyeballing Roger's diagram we'd probably conclude that:

- The minimum to stay competitive is at the peak of the bell curve (the 50% mark), so it's fine if I do it right as we cross into Late Majority.
- To materially outperform the competition, I should adopt technology before the early majority in my industry (i.e., with the innovators or early adopters).

But this is only somewhat helpful because all it's doing is telling you that in general, you want to be on the left side of the graph. To get a more complete view of this, we need to factor in risk.

Let's look at curves of the overall adoption of technology, and the risk that it entails:

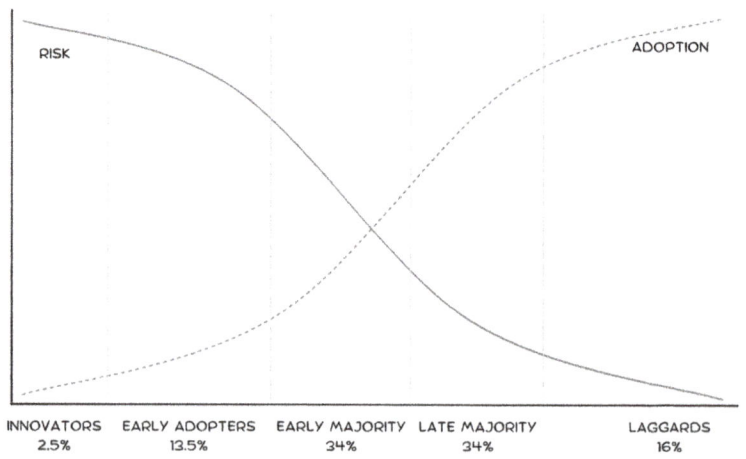

| INNOVATORS | EARLY ADOPTERS | EARLY MAJORITY | LATE MAJORITY | LAGGARDS |
|---|---|---|---|---|
| 2.5% | 13.5% | 34% | 34% | 16% |

In the above visual, we see that as the adoption of a technology increases, the risk decreases. That's because more widely adopted technologies have had more of the kinks ironed out, there's a wider base of support for them, and company staff understands how to use them.

Back to what we're trying to accomplish: we want to *outperform* the competition. For our specific competitor group, we need to be better at picking how far to the left or right of the adoption/ risk graph we want to be *for our situation*.

If we consistently make better decisions, even if some of the decisions don't go in our favor, in the aggregate we have an edge.

A friend who used to play poker professionally explained the concept well. In poker, no player can win every hand. What professionals do is carefully calculate the expected value (EV) of each hand to *make a positive return over the long term*. They make decisions based on what's mathematically profitable (+EV) at any given time – even if the cards they're holding don't look like they would win a hand.

Similarly, a company considering new technology shouldn't only focus on avoiding risk for a single technology choice. To beat the competition, it should adopt a strategy of picking a point on the adoption curve that gives a positive Expected Value (+EV) in the long run. This might mean investing in a technology during the "Innovators" or "Early Adopters" stage, despite the apparent risk and uncertainty.

# The Psychology of Risk-Taking

Taking risks with new technologies feels uncomfortable, particularly if you're not a "techy" type. Even if using your logical brain you know taking an appropriate level of risk will yield a positive return, the world is conspiring to scare you off of sticking with that strategy. Let's look at why.

First, the media. If you haven't already done yourself a favor and instituted a news blackout, at least understand that perspectives you see on mass media will conspire to scare you from taking smart bets. Their incentive is to drive advertising revenue. They don't drive revenue by catering to a small minority of people at the cutting edge of technology. Instead, they play to the late majority and laggards, sensationalizing volatility at the cutting edge or scaring people from what could be a promising future.

Second, financial bubbles. I mentioned Carlota Perez's *Technological Revolutions and Financial Capital* earlier. She describes how new technologies attract outsized interest when they are still more speculative, leading to a financial bubble. When a financial bubble pops, people have the mistaken idea that the underlying investment area (the technology) is dead – which as I noted earlier isn't the case. It could still be incredibly useful to you, regardless of whether speculators have overinvested in it or gone bust doing so.

To help protect from making emotionally driven decisions, watch for these phases of market psychology – **all of which have nothing to do with whether a technology is +EV for you**:

- **Skepticism**: "This technology is just a fad, it won't go anywhere."
- **Greed**: "This could be the Next Big Thing! Get in now!"
- **Fear**: "A bunch of people lost their shirt investing in it. The tech is dead, let's move on."
- **Opportunity**: "It looks like there actually is something to this, let's give it another shot."
- **Acceptance**: "This technology is a part of what we do day to day."

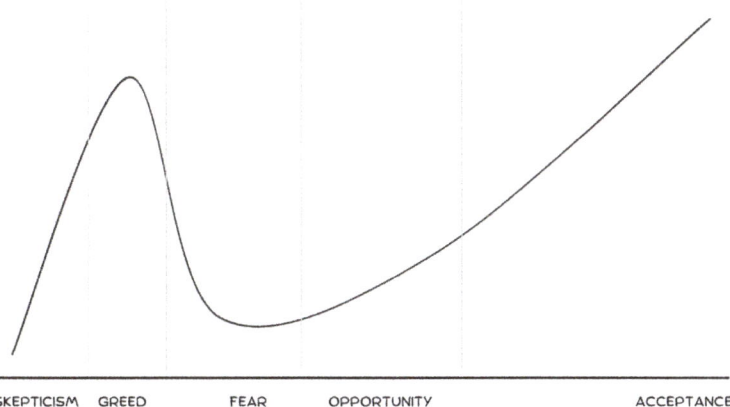

SKEPTICISM   GREED        FEAR        OPPORTUNITY                    ACCEPTANCE

Different parts of the market, different competitors, and different media might be at various points in this progression. And it doesn't matter where they are. What matters is that you are seeing they are expressing an *emotional* reaction (which can drive investing FOMO) – and shouldn't be the driver of your decision whether to adopt a technology.

Remember, your goal is to build the best machine. Adopting technology is a risk-reward decision for a given *process*. If you've defined your process outputs well, and understand the exceptions which could occur and their magnitude, you have a good basis for making a choice.

# 3.8

# How To Choose Your Risk Profile

We're trying to determine how early you can adopt a technology for a given process within risks that are acceptable to your business. We've established that your long-term competitive edge is determined by making smarter decisions on risk/reward, and you shouldn't be scared off by what the outside world thinks.

How can you decide how early to install a new technology into a process? For this, we can go back to our friend, Expected Value. I wish there was a clear-cut, numbers-driven formula for this, but there isn't.

However, going through this exercise with even directional data[4] will give you an edge over the competition – because they're just running around making guesses based on fear and greed, and not thinking in a logical framework.

---

4   I have a ton of free resources on using directional data in my Scientific Entrepreneurship resources on my personal site, rajjha.com

Here's how you can make a directional EV decision for each new technology you are considering installing in a process:

## Step 1: Assess the Potential Payoff

Because you understand the costs in the current process (they're in the *logs*), you have a baseline. Estimate the potential enterprise value that adoption could add. This could be in reduced cost, improved products, improved operational efficiency, etc. In essence, make a guesstimate as to how much benefit you'll get for adopting this technology.

A simple example for any business: your marketing manager Sally costs $40/hour. One of her responsibilities is writing blog posts. You peek into the logs for this process and find each post takes 1 hour to research and outline, 3 hours to write and edit, and 1 hour to SEO optimize and post to the blog and create links to other posts, or $200. Using the most basic AI tool it cuts the writing and editing time down from 3 hours to 0.5 hours. You just saved $100 per blog post, or $10,400 per year if they're being done twice per week. If you dug a little deeper, you could likely replace $160 ($16,640 annually). But wait, this means Sally also gained back 208 hours per year! Now she can do outreach, set up meetings with partners – all those things you never get around to. You mock up some processes for those … and it looks like the outputs for those could generate $50,000 in new business.

… and this is just getting started. You realize you can do the same thing for your newsletter. And website copy. And customer support…

Don't include pie-in-the-sky payoffs "If this goes well we'll be a $10B company" – focus on things that are more than 1% likely to be true.

The short of it is, add up all the benefits. That's your Potential Payoff.

## Step 2: Assess Probability of Success

Next, you'll make a guesstimate as to your odds of success. This won't be scientific, just directional. Think through the following:

- How mature is the technology? Are there examples of others doing this today (even if in different industries)?
- Do I have the resources in-house to do this? If not, add those to the list in Step 3. If yes, do I think I can motivate them to deploy this technology quickly?
- Will I get internal resistance? Will that impact the odds of success? (refer to the chapter "The One Hour Unlock" for a script to help this)

Ask these kinds of questions to get your odds of success. It could be 90%, 73%, 1%... The point is you've thought about it and assigned it a value you think is reasonable. Save this list, you'll add it to your *exception* handling if you install the technology.

In the simple example of enabling Sally with AI tools, in my experience, the odds of success are exceedingly high, and the downsides are low.

## Step 3: Assess Potential Costs/Risks

Time to think about the bad stuff. What are the costs and risks associated with adopting the technology?

- What does the technology cost (including people to install and operate it)?
- If the technology breaks, what are the consequences?
- Are there regulatory concerns that will cost the company money?

These questions get to what kinds of things can go wrong.

Don't include things where a simple operational fix could handle it. For example, the issue I had years ago of a writer plagiarizing written material – very damaging, but could be prevented by adding an automated copyright check when each written piece was done.

Also don't include things that are less than 1% likely to happen (like HAL-9000 not opening the airlock and leaving you to die). To simplify things we're cropping off the super unlikely good and bad scenarios since our brains are bad at estimating odds for big-magnitude things.

## Step 4: Assess Probability of Failure

You guessed it, now we're going to estimate the probability that the costs and risks we listed in step 3 will actually happen.

## Step 5: Calculate Expected Value

Now it's time to calculate your rough expected value:

Expected Value = (Probability of Success × Potential Payoff) – (Probability of Failure × Potential Loss)

If the EV you calculated above is positive, go for it.

You have a choice right now. You can be like Kodak, Blockbuster, or thousands of other companies, big and small, who waited on the technology because it was 'too hard,' were protecting yesterday's profits at the expense of tomorrow's, or didn't make a dispassionate calculation of the value of new technology.

# 3.∞

# The Zero Person Company?

I made a plan for a Zero Person Company run by AI.

It didn't work.

But it will.

Here's why.

AI is pretty remarkable. At this point, it can handle most customer service issues. Generate marketing creative. Run ad campaigns. Order products. Manage inventory.

I had an idea for a zero-person company in 2012. This was long before any of this tech was available, and while I was fixated on it for a long time and sketched out dozens of automations, I mothballed it as impractical. I revived it in 2023 when AI finally got good enough that it might be possible.

I started playing with AI agents. Individual AI's aren't quite good enough for doing everything in a business... They'll still screw up and do something bizarre once in a while. However, an AI agent can delegate to or supervise the output of another AI.

Remember how we discussed the idea that humans expect deterministic robots (robots that follow set rules), but most AIs in use today are probabilistic (good guessers)?

What if I had an AI supervise another AI? Now there's another layer of certainty.

Or is there?

Turns out, only kinda – because neither the supervisor nor the worker are predictable. Usually, only small things go wrong, but sometimes problems will pile on other mistakes, and off it goes to a bizarre result.

Just like we saw that a 0.01% error rate from one AI can compound into big mistakes over time, the same can happen with agents supervising AIs.

But it can get even worse.

That's because it's not just one kind of error compounding, it's multiple different systems each with its own unpredictable errors. So even if the odds aren't high, you have the possibility of something going wildly off track.

And human employees? Don't *they* make mistakes? Well, they're messy – but (cults aside) they tend not to compound each others' mistakes.

An AI might issue a customer a discount code … get asked for a bigger one by the customer … not know what to do with that and escalate it to its AI supervisor … who then gives a promise of free products for life when it misinterprets the customer email as a threat of lawsuit.

There are SO MANY edge cases where things can go wrong. It's not that AIs can't handle them, it's that (as of now) there's an incompatibility with what we're REALLY trying to do running a company.

**This is a big and important reframe.** Most people are so busy asking what they can automate, that they're not asking the right question. There's something bigger at play here.

A business exists to *create value for its owners*. It takes in capital and creates assets and cashflows. The second predictability goes down, the business is worth less (to the owner, or to a buyer).

And if unpredictability is too high, it's worthless. As you saw in the chapter "Mo' Money," a huge part of what business buyers pay is based on risk.

Today, and in the immediate future, AIs aren't quite good enough for creating predictability in many decisions. With the robots in charge, my business might be worth $0 in five minutes. For now, at least, the robots make great factory floor workers. With bumpers on what they can and cannot do. They make great thinking partners for you. But they aren't ready to be in charge.

Sure, I can have agents watching the agents. But that doesn't solve the problem. Because they can talk themselves into a bizarre corner.

**And I'm not going to build a financial asset with a bomb in it.**

So we're back to having guardrails, which are human-monitored.

No Zero Person Company today.

Mind you, I think we'll get there. And I'll keep tinkering at the workbench. But as of now, an important lesson: if you own a company keep your eye on what really matters – predictability.

# EPILOGUE

You've just read a book, the first two Parts of which are timeless – but portions of the last Part were obsolete the day after I wrote it. The world is moving too fast for any writing on the state of automation & AI to stay current for long. To that end, I've prepared resources for you to stay up to date.

You can find those at <u>TheBusinessUnlock.com/resources</u>.

## Before You Go –

A lot went into making this book (zero words written by AI, I'm old-school). I hope you got as much or more out of it.

I'd sincerely appreciate if you would leave an honest review of it here: <u>TheBusinessUnlock.com/review</u>

# ABOUT THE AUTHOR

Raj Jha is a 5-time company founder, former public company executive, and former attorney. He has personally negotiated over $440 million in sales transactions and spent 17+ years advising companies such as Facebook, Yahoo, Electronic Arts, and Polycom. Raj has overseen the creation of over 753 strategic plans for companies in multiple industries.

Raj's goal is to help entrepreneurs achieve personal autonomy by understanding the algorithms of business.

You can find out more at rajjha.com